HOW T
FIVE-MINU

C000076362

Other Allison & Busby Writers' Guides

HOW TO WRITE FIVE-MINUTE FEATURES

Alison Chisholm

a&b

This edition published in Great Britain in 1997 by
Allison & Busby Ltd
114 New Cavendish Street
London W1M 7FD

First published in Great Britain in 1995 by
Allison & Busby

A catalogue record for this book is available from
the British Library.

ISBN 0 74900 203 4

Designed and typeset by N-J Design Associates
Romsey, Hampshire
Printed and bound in Great Britain by
WBC Book Manufacturers Ltd
Bridgend, Mid Glamorgan

CONTENTS

1

INTRODUCTION

Short pieces of writing can be produced in odd moments. They are fun to do, and they provide the writer with two tangible rewards in the form of regular publication and the accompanying small sums of cash. They fall into five main categories.

Definitions

- A reader's letter is directed to the editor of a newspaper or magazine. It is intended for publication on a page devoted to the thoughts, ideas, brief anecdotes and opinions of readers who wish to share them with other readers.
- A filler is a short piece designed to occupy a space left by the main bulk of text on a page. It may be an interesting fact, a tip, an anecdote, a joke, a puzzle – in fact, anything which fills the page and adds to the pleasingly busy look of the paper or magazine.
- A 'short-short' article is any non-fiction piece of up to around 400 words. There is no strictly defined limit for these, however, and different editors would describe different lengths of work as 'short-shorts'. They are frequently solicited by a magazine editor on a set theme, eg. 'Our Town', 'It Changed my Life' or 'Soapbox'. These are the longest pieces considered in this book. For detailed information on producing longer features, consult 'The Craft of Writing Articles' by Gordon Wells (Allison and Busby).

- Ultra-short fiction is defined here as any piece of fiction complete in under 500 words.
- A slogan is a phrase which makes an immediate impact in a few words. Advertisers know the value of a catchy saying which becomes synonymous with a product. For the freelance writer, these brief, memorable phrases are usually devised with the hope of competition success.

For the purposes of this book, the above will be referred to collectively as 'shorts'.

Shorts are not easy to write. They demand a lively imagination with a constant fund of new ideas. They require a keen sense of observation, an ability to get to the essential nugget of information without waffle, and a tautly controlled skill in the manipulation of words. These attributes are vital for every writer, and writing shorts is the best possible method of honing the skills.

Some writers make the mistake of overlooking the potential in shorts. When you hear them being discussed, you will hear all of the following sad comments:

'I used to do them when I started. I've moved on now.' This statement implies that shorts are a basic training ground for writers. Having mastered the skills required, they see no purpose in pursuing this style of writing.

'They are too bitty. You can't get your teeth into them.' True – if you are only going to produce one short at a sitting. A session of writing them, producing six . . . ten . . . even twenty pieces at one go is more rewarding. The added bonus is that your imagination flows more readily with every one you produce. It might take a few minutes to come up with your first idea, but that first one turns on the tap which encourages the surge of ideas for all the rest.

'Who ever gets remembered for readers' letters?' Probably nobody. The nature of shorts is that they have momentary appeal. They allow the reader a quick smile, a flash of fellow-feeling, an instant's irritation – and then he or she moves on to the next piece. If you are seeking immortality, write the definitive novel, or the poem which changes the world. If you want to amuse, inform or entertain, keep up your output of shorts.

'I'm too professional to bother with them.' If being professional means producing a high standard of work, the

length of the piece of writing is immaterial. Professionalism is as important in the short as it is in the blockbuster saga or the hour-long television documentary. If being professional means writing for money, be sure to select paying outlets for letters.

'They don't earn enough to interest a serious writer.' A single published letter will not provide you with a second home or a month in the Bahamas. Keep writing them, and even with a good acceptance rate, you will not be able to consider early retirement. See them as a source of pin-money and you may be surprised to note how quickly the sums add up.

Think about the rate of pay in relation to the length of a short. A reader's letter will provide you with only a few pounds – but for just a few words. If a letter of 25 words brings payment of £10, you are looking at a rate of £400 per 1,000 words. The situation begins to appear healthier.

One thought to consider: the tiny sums involved in payment for individual shorts will disappear if they are deposited in the domestic bank account. Keep a separate account for them, and take Scrooge-like pleasure from watching the sums accrue. A target purchase, such as a word processor, a weekend break or some little personal extravagance, will spur you on to keep adding to the fund.

Time Management and Efficiency

This heading may appear to belong to a manual on business practice rather than to a volume on writing; but the writer is a busy person. The successful writer is just as concerned with streamlining output and working to maximum efficiency as any business manager.

If you are producing nothing but shorts, plan your writing time in terms of slots for market study, research, exploring ideas, actual typing and preparing submissions. This means juggling several different ideas at any one time, finding outlets for them all at once, typing them at the same time, etc. By doing this you will make far more efficient use of the hours available than if you took each idea individually and carried it through all of its different stages.

For most writers, however, shorts will not be the only form of writing being undertaken. Whether you choose to specialise in a particular genre, or float butterfly-fashion from article to short story to full-length book and back, you will always have slots in your writing life into which shorts could be inserted.

You may be fitting your writing into spaces between other jobs. If this is the case, you will almost certainly have odd gaps of fifteen minutes or so for which you have not accounted. A gap of this length would hardly allow you time to make inroads into your full-length work, but it is ideal for producing a short.

You may be writing as a full-time career. If so, it might be helpful to start the day with a couple of shorts in order to warm yourself up for the weight of work ahead of you.

You may find that domestic circumstances dictate the hours in the day available for your writing. Perhaps you can only get your teeth into your work late at night, when the children are in bed, or early in the day, before you have to start caring for an invalid or elderly person. If this is so, the tiny spaces of time when the baby takes an afternoon nap or the invalid is resting quietly are ideal for producing shorts.

It is a good idea to write down a detailed timetable for your week, highlighting all the writing times available to you. Then go back over your timetable marking those additional areas of even just a few minutes which would allow you enough time to write a short.

Some magazine editors are willing to consider legibly handwritten readers' letters. One useful stratagem is to carry a writing pad and envelopes with you at all times. You can squeeze the most efficient use from your time by whipping out the pad and creating a reader's letter while waiting for the bus or during your tea break.

Whether you are able to produce letters in this way or not, cultivate the habit of carrying pen and paper with you at all times. You can guarantee that the idea for a filler, the hilarious overheard remark or the perfect verse for a greetings card will strike you at the most inconvenient moment. If you cannot capture the idea on paper at the minute of its conception, you may lose it for ever.

Jot it down at once and it is preserved, ready for the time when you will be able to give it your undivided attention. Working through the list of ideas you have accumulated in the past few days has the added bonus of making the most efficient use of your typing time.

Shorts and the Novice Writer

Shorts are an ideal introduction to the craft of writing. By their nature, they are quick to produce; so a newcomer to writing, working far more slowly than an experienced practitioner, can still complete a piece at one sitting.

Although a rejection of any kind is hurtful, a rejected short stings less than an unwanted novel or story. After all, your personal investment in its creation amounts to no more than a little bit of thought and a brief period of time. You have neither poured your entire creative genius into it, nor laboured over it for months.

There is a large market for shorts, and so, statistically, a good chance of success. Most newspapers print a page of readers' letters each day. Magazines may print twelve or fifteen letters a week, compared with, perhaps, just one story or a couple of articles.

One of the most frustrating things about starting to write is the dearth of feedback. It seems to take forever to receive a verdict on your *magnum opus*. And as soon as the despair or euphoria has dissipated, you have to start waiting again. If you are writing shorts, you will soon establish a pipeline of submissions. This gives you a reason to watch for the postman.

An acceptance or the cheque in payment for a letter which has been published lifts you up, and you are bolstered by the knowledge that the next day may bring still more good news. A rejection does not hurt quite so much when you reflect that there are still twenty submissions 'doing the rounds', and any one of those might bring you a change of luck. You are unlikely to go for very long without getting some sort of feedback.

Shorts and the Experienced Writer

In addition to writing a couple of shorts at the beginning of the day, an experienced writer may find shorts the ideal way to unwind when the main work of the day is over.

The psychological lift of an acceptance is as great for the experienced writer as it is for the novice, since needing an incentive to watch for the postman is vital to all writers, regardless of how long they have been practising their craft. It helps to sweeten the pill of the occasional but inevitable rejection. It reminds the writer that there is a world outside, and one in which writing is still being recognised and published.

Producing shorts is an excellent way of overcoming writer's block. It can also, in between bursts of work on the major project, refresh the palate jaded by labouring for hours over the masterpiece.

The most important factor, however, is that shorts pull on the writer's rein with their insistence on conciseness and precision. They quell any tendency to waffle or pad. They require plain language used in a conversational idiom. They need to communicate with total clarity.

2

READERS' LETTERS

Most of the shorts appearing in print are readers' letters, and it is important for the writer to explore this form in detail.

By reading as many letter pages as you can find, you will absorb a tremendous amount of general information concerning appropriate subject matter and style.

Market Study

After acquiring general information about letter pages, you need to concentrate on the specific requirements of individual publications. For letters to the editor to be accepted, they must be appropriate to their target market. The only way to establish their suitability is to study the markets, looking at three particular aspects of each potential outlet.

- Consider the editorial style. Is the outlet chatty, formal, sarcastic, witty? A chatty publication is less likely than a formal one to take a starchy, businesslike letter.
- What sort of advertisements appear in your target outlet? If they are for business equipment, management seminars etc., the readership is unlikely to be interested in a humorous verse about your cat. If they are for mobility aids and arthritis remedies, your clever tips about washing babyclothes are inappropriate.
- Look particularly at the letters page. For each piece printed there, ask yourself why it was successful. Whether you think it is good or indifferent, challenging or banal does not matter: the fact is, it was selected for publication.

For every letters page you study, make notes of the number of pieces featured and their average length. Write brief details of their content, noting whether they are controversial, deferential, anecdotal, etc. Try to look at the same publication over a number of issues. You will almost certainly see an emerging pattern.

This market study has a double advantage for the writer. It gives you a clear picture of the requirements of a magazine or newspaper, so that you will be able to angle your piece precisely to meet those requirements. It also introduces you to the range of approaches found on different letters pages. If, therefore, you have a specific message which must be put across in a certain way for maximum impact, your study will direct your pre-written piece into its most likely route to acceptance.

When considering the magazine markets, do start by consulting the excellent biennial 'Magazine Writer's Handbook' (Allison and Busby). In this, Gordon Wells provides an invaluable listing of the more general markets for letters, fillers and other shorts. But remember, the handbook provides only initial guidance. You will still need to do your own detailed, up-to-date market research.

National Newspapers

The national press offers you a chance to comment on news events. This is where you can mount any personal soapbox to put your side of an argument. You can air your views on British or international politics, the world situation, or the fact that you have heard the first cuckoo of Spring.

Newspapers give you the perfect platform for attracting attention to a cause or an injustice. Their distribution ensures that readers all over the country will have an opportunity to learn your views, and an equal platform for agreeing or disagreeing with you.

The range of material you can submit is as broad as the range of newspapers published. Remember that the same news stories will be carried by a number of papers in entirely different ways.

The Times and the *Daily Mirror* may offer information on the same subject. The facts may be identical, but the manner of their presentation will be very different. Just as the journalistic style varies from one paper to another, so your letter style should reflect the same variation. A letter suitable for *The Times* is unlikely to fit into the *Daily Mirror*, and vice versa.

On the question of payment, you will find that the more highbrow papers are less likely to pay for readers' letters than the popular press. Some papers send prizes in return for letters rather than cash.

Do check the national papers thoroughly for every letter opening they offer. In addition to the main letters page, several have occasional features where readers' opinions are solicited on a specific topic. They may have a page devoted to letters concerned with sport. They may seek out readers' solutions to other readers' problems. Each of these pages is a potential outlet for your writing, which will allow you some personal publicity and impose on you the discipline of writing on a set theme – a very useful exercise.

Local Newspapers

The local press offers you an opportunity to express your views on any local subject. Less global in its concerns than the national papers, your neighbourhood newspaper is likely to provide essential reading for the people in your town. Your letter printed there may not make an impact at the opposite end of the country, but will be seen and studied by those to whom it is relevant.

Council decisions, closure of local amenities, potholes in the road and parking regulations will all feature in letters pages. Be controversial; start an argument and then stand back and be amazed by the heat it generates.

Write regularly to your paper and you will establish a relationship with other contributors. The less cordial this relationship, the better. A correspondent who disagrees with your views will help to make the letters page more interesting for the casual reader, who will start to turn to that page first, and will read and absorb all your opinions. Controversial responses will lead to a more thorough consideration of the issue.

It is unusual to receive payment for letters in these

publications. See the appearance of your letter as an opportunity to put your point across, knowing that it will reach its target readership.

There may be a spin-off effect from this form of letter writing. Local papers often prefer to use knowledgeable correspondents to cover specific areas of interest, rather than their own staff. If you wanted to provide copy about the Chess Club, Horticultural Society etc., you would already have shown your commitment and interest through your contributions to the letters page. It is not too large a step from there to providing specimen news features in these specialised areas. Do them well enough, and you could end up with a regular column.

Special Interest Magazines

There are publications devoted to every interest and leisure pursuit you can think of, and doubtless to some you have never even considered. Many of these areas of interest spawn a wide range of magazines. Go into any large newsagent's to see how many titles concern computers, needlework or childcare. Think of a minority sphere of interest, and you may still find a choice of magazines.

Compare the letters pages of various titles on a given day, starting with a subject which is dear to your own heart. (It is always more interesting for you as a writer and for your potential readers if you can write with unforced enthusiasm.)

You may find that one magazine takes a narrow and scholarly approach to a subject; another considers a broad area of interest tangential to the central subject; one contains nothing but comment on features which have appeared in previous issues; another uses lighthearted material.

Through this study, you will have discovered how to prepare your material and direct it most effectively into each outlet. Establish a rapport with a range of magazines devoted to your target special interest, and you are establishing yourself as an authority. This is a valuable exercise.

Special interest magazines, however large their circulation, appeal by their nature to a minority of readers. Only a fraction of that minority will be corresponding with the magazine. Regular correspondents will become known and noticed. Theirs will be the names that spring to mind if the editor wishes to solicit freelance material. You can insert a useful foot in the door by ensuring that your name is never far from the editor's mind or letters page.

It is logical to submit to magazines dedicated to your own special interest, but remember that you can always expand your spheres of interest. Start by considering all the topics which have ever had any relevance in your life. You enjoy cooking? Look at cookery magazines. You follow a football team? Consider magazines devoted to that sport. You have been on a diet, made a chest of drawers, enjoyed watching television? Look through the dieting, DIY and programme listings magazines.

When you have exhausted the areas where you have some knowledge, you have still not reached the end of the road. Instead, look at the publications devoted to subjects which do not interest you at all. You may never have felt inclined to climb a mountain, buy a used car or give birth; but the magazines aimed at those who do feel so inclined still offer outlets for your letters.

Such advice would be suspect if the subject of this book were full-length articles. The beauty of writing shorts is that a fractional amount of knowledge, a second-hand anecdote or sometimes mere curiosity is all that is required.

There is just one word of warning. Not all special interest magazines pay for letters they print, and of those which do, some pay in kind rather than in cash. Be sure you know what to expect. One former gardener loved to read all the relevant publications, but latterly had only a tiny window box to enjoy. Her letter to a gardening magazine was rewarded with a huge bale of peat moss, so heavy she could scarcely struggle it into the lift of her block of flats.

General Interest Magazines

This category should perhaps have read 'Women's Magazines', as there are few general interest publications which are not targeted at a female readership. They represent a huge paying market for letters which are chatty and casual.

Almost every women's magazine has a busy letters page which reflects all aspects of women's lives. Male writers should not find this offputting. The man's observation is welcomed, too.

Some pages regularly reserve a column for letters on a specific theme, eg. household tips or overheard remarks. Others jumble the different styles of letter together, giving the reader a 'lucky dip' of topics. Some add colour and interest by printing contributors' photographs.

The next chapter offers a list of the sort of topics featured in this broadest area of letter pages, and gives examples of the various types.

Perhaps because they provide the largest outlet for paid letters, women's magazines receive them in vast numbers. Competition is fierce. Do not let this put you off. Good letters will always find their niche. In a market area as large as this, there are second, third, fourth and further choices of outlet for letters which were not accepted when first offered.

This range of outlets makes the letter (and filler) unique. An article or short story tailored to one magazine could seldom be sent to another without considerable rewriting. The letter which has not been used can be submitted elsewhere in its original form (provided that you have allowed sufficient time to elapse to ensure that it remains unpublished).

Writing Style and Layout

The key factor to remember when writing a reader's letter is concision. By its nature, a letter must make its point in a few words. Even a longer letter (and your market study will have shown which publications take longer material) allows no room for extraneous matter. Be as chatty and casual as you can.

When you are writing, keep to the point. Make your sentences short, without too many subclauses which might confuse. Do not spend time introducing your topic gradually; launch straight into it. There is no need for any preamble. State your subject clearly, and do not attempt to cover additional subjects. They are the material for further letters.

12

Submit just one letter at a time, and allow time to pass before you send further work to the same outlet. Be sure that you never send letters at shorter intervals than the frequency of publication of the periodical, ie. allow a month to elapse at the very least before sending another letter to the same monthly magazine.

The presentation of letters is a little different from standard manuscript presentation. You do not need to submit a covering letter and provide a coversheet of information giving your address and telephone number, as you would for an article or story.

Instead you set out your letter to the editor just as you would any other letter. This example of a simple domestic incident (which was published and paid for by a women's magazine) demonstrates:

21 Any Street
Anytown
Anywhere
13th April

Dear Editor

My daughters had been to stay with their grandparents for a few days, and were full of excitement about their visit. I asked what they had enjoyed most. 'Getting washed,' the younger one replied. 'Grandma only ASKED us if we'd done the back of our necks – she didn't know she had to look to make sure.'

Yours sincerely

A. Williams

You will note that the term 'Dear Editor' is used. Again, this device is a little different from the formula you would use if submitting an article or story. In that case, the courtesy of quoting the editor's name in the covering letter would be appreciated.

Note, too, that the letter is signed and the address given. If your letter tackles an embarrassing or controversial subject, most editors will withhold your name and address on request, but they should always be given as a matter of course.

N.B. The reader's letter is the only form of manuscript which may be submitted to a publication without the courtesy of enclosing a stamped, self-addressed envelope. If, however, you expect an acknowledgement or the return of a photograph, the s.a.e. is necessary.

Further Points on Presentation

When preparing the material for this book, I approached a number of editors of women's magazines, and asked them various questions with regard to readers' letters. I am indebted to those editors who took the time and trouble to reply.

The replies, however, presented me with a problem. I had hoped to sum up their comments and offer a universally acceptable formula for submitting letters. Unfortunately this will be impossible, as the requirements varied so much.

Indeed, there is little point in quoting the requirements of any individual magazine. A change of editor could mean a change of policy, and the information would be out of date as you read it.

You will be on generally safe ground if you follow these guidelines.

- For preference, type your manuscript – but very neat handwriting or block capital printing can be offered.
- Do not attempt to hoodwink the editor. Writing each week in a different persona is unacceptable. Write from your own viewpoint, and if you wish to use a pseudonym, always use the same one.
- You do not need to supply a title for a letter. Titles are selected by the magazine staff.

One point of special interest arising from the survey concerned a specimen letter. It was laid out in the format of the example given above, which was regarded as universally acceptable.

Some editors were kind enough to comment on the content of the letter. The same sample had been sent to them all, and was an anecdotal letter of my own which had already been published. Comments ranged from 'Just the sort of thing we would use' to 'Unbelievable ... unfunny ... wouldn't use it.'

There is just one editor, who shall remain anonymous, whose comments are not included in the information given above. This editor sent back my explanatory letter, questionnaire and sample reader's letter with a pro forma reply. The reply thanked me for sending the enclosed short story, but stated that they would not be able to use it in the magazine. I was wished luck in placing it elsewhere.

There are two important messages in these last points. One is to remember the saying that 'One man's meat is another man's poison.' Do not despair if your letter is ignored or rejected. Somebody, somewhere will love it as much as you do.

The second is that, with the best will in the world, editors are fallible human beings. It was obvious that nobody had even glanced at my material before it was returned with a totally inappropriate response. It can be inferred, then, that the rejection of any piece could be the result of somebody's inattention or lack of care.

The moral of this is never to let a rejection affect you on a personal level. A piece of writing which fails to find its niche is a hiccup in the job. It is of no more significance than the plumber's periodical leaky joint or the doctor's occasional patient who fails to respond. (But writer, plumber or doctor – if there are too many hiccups, take the hint and re-examine your technique!)

Keeping Records

This may not be the most exciting part of the job, but it is essential. As soon as you start to submit letters on a regular basis, set up a filing system to keep track of them.

This is not, perhaps, so important if your letters are one-off communications to newspapers. But if you are hoping to set up a network of correspondence to magazine letters pages, you will need a foolproof system for checking.

You will be surprised to realise how quickly you can forget the date and destination of your letters, even when you have only submitted a few. By the time you have fifty in the pipeline, relying on memory is impossible.

Experience will help you to work out which is the most appropriate method of keeping records for you. This basic system is simple to operate, and a good way to start.

Each time you write a letter, take an exact, dated copy of it – your record copy. Send the letter to the magazine of your choice and write the magazine's name on your record copy. Place the record copy in an ordinary wallet folder.

With every new submission you will have a new record copy to add to the file. Store them face upwards underneath those already in place. You will end up with a pile of record copies dated in chronological order. The one at the top of the pile will be the one you sent out first.

As a double check, it is a good idea to keep in an exercise book a list of the topics of each of your letters, its destination, and the date it was submitted. Leave a column for making a note of the outcome.

From time to time, go through your file removing the record copy of any letter which has been published. Take out, too, those letters which were submitted several months before but have not appeared in print. You will be left with only your most recent submissions.

There is one essential factor to bear in mind when you are resubmitting letters. Magazines are looking for original material, and will not publish letters which have already appeared in print. So be sure to allow a considerable time to elapse before offering your work elsewhere. If you fail to do this, you run the risk of severe embarrassment by having a letter appear in one magazine when you have already sent it to another for consideration.

Allow an editor at least six months to use your letter in a publication which appears weekly. Give ten months for a monthly magazine, and, at the very least, a year for a quarterly.

If an appropriate period of time has gone by, make a fresh copy of your letter and send it to another magazine. Add the name of this second magazine to your record copy, and make a note of the date of submission. Place the record copy at the bottom of the pile in your folder, and update your exercise book.

Repeat the process as often as you need to with unpublished letters, remembering that there may be a dozen or so dates and destinations noted before the record copy can be transferred to an 'accepted' file.

16

This 'accepted' file provides you with your record of published letters. It is helpful if you can add a copy of the magazine in which each letter appeared. Compare your original with the printed version. Any differences you note between them provide you with useful information about the magazine's preferred style. If your sentences have been shortened, or words altered, bear in mind the changes made the next time you are writing to that magazine. The closer your letter is to approved house style, the more likely it is that it will be accepted.

Do not be too disappointed if you cannot locate the magazines where your letters have appeared. Most publications do not warn you in advance when your work is to be used. Your first intimation of its acceptance may be the cheque which arrives a few weeks after the letter was printed.

Remember that your cheque will be made out in the name under which you submitted your letter. If you are using a pseudonym, be sure to advise your bank of this, or there may be problems when you present the cheque. A brief word of explanation, and possibly the signing of an indemnity form, will ensure that you have no difficulties in the future.

Magazine editors would obviously prefer their contributors to buy regular copies. This is impractical, especially if you are sending work out to twenty or more publications. Keep a check on the letters pages in a range of magazines by browsing through them in your largest local newsagent's. Play the game by buying a title or two to keep the shop staff – and editors – happy.

3

TYPES OF LETTERS

The idea behind a reader's letter to a magazine is different from the idea behind an epic. It is slight, fleeting and uncomplicated. If you cannot sum up your letter idea in a single sentence, it is too complex for its intended form. Think about producing it as a story or article, or subdividing it into a number of different letters.

There will always be days when the ideas refuse to flow. The suggestion has already been made that you should keep a notebook for observations, tips and 'overheards'. Reading through this is bound to get the creative juices flowing.

It may also help you to marshal your thoughts if you think in terms of categories of women's magazine letter. The list below gives ten letter categories, and then each is explained with examples:

- comment
- controversy
- information
- humorous anecdotes
- family anecdotes
- confused sayings
- tips
- overheards
- verse
- observations

Comment

In this letter, you refer back to anything which has appeared in a recent past issue of the magazine. You may be endorsing or disagreeing with an article, offering a new viewpoint or opening up a subject for further discussion.

Imagine that a feature had appeared on the subject of banning smoking from offices. A 'comment' letter from you might say:

> In the July issue Jane Smith wrote to condemn the practice of smoking in an office environment. Smoking is an addiction, not a leisure activity. Would she be as quick to condemn fellow workers who used prescribed tranquilisers, or who took a drink during their lunchbreak?

Or you might put:

> I agree strongly with Jane Smith and her assertion that smoking should be banned from offices. I am asthmatic, and have suffered severe discomfort thanks to the selfishness of smokers. It is time that legislation controlled this antisocial habit.

In each of these examples, you are commenting directly on the subject of the article. If you followed a different tack, your letter would have more originality value, eg:

> It was interesting to note that the July issue carried a long article on the perils of smoking in offices. Why, then, were three different cigarette advertisements featured in the magazine.

Although these letters are specifically geared to the magazine where the original piece appeared, the first two examples still have validity as letters. If the target magazine does not print them, simple adaptation of the wording would make them appropriate for submission as controversial letters to another magazine. For example, you might open with 'On the question of whether smoking should be allowed in offices . . .' or 'I believe the time has come to ban smoking in all offices'.

19

Controversy

Open up an area for debate among the readers of a letters page, and you are creating an additional outlet for other writers to use.

You may feel very strongly about a topic and wish to have your say. You may merely want to open the argument, and have no strong feelings either way. If this is the case, come down on the side you think will create the stronger reaction against your letter. For example:

> It has become fashionable to deplore the use of smacking as a punishment for small children. I believe that if more children were smacked, there would be fewer teenage delinquents. Do other readers agree?

You are thus leaving the door wide open for comeback on both sides of the argument.

One thing to remember in controversial writing is that there is always a gap between submission and publication of the letter. The example quoted here is a perennial question. There would be no point in opening up an argument on a current news item. Do that in a letter to the daily press.

Information

You can use magazine letters pages to disseminate information to others, or to attract information you need, as in these examples:

> Did you know that this year marks a special anniversary for the Society of Friends of the Vietnamese Pot-Bellied Pig? Why not share in the celebrations by sponsoring a pig, and learning more about these fascinating creatures?

Or to gain information:

> I am writing a book about the rise and fall in popularity of Church Youth Clubs. Did you belong to a Youth Club? How often did you meet? Did you make special friends, or perhaps meet your life partner there? Please write to me at the address given with any information which could be included. All letters will be answered, and your anonymity is guaranteed.

The informative letter can also be used to share a good idea:

My daughter has taken part in various sponsored events over the years in order to help raise money for charity. Most of these have involved going for walks or learning spellings, providing interest perhaps, but no practical benefit. So it was good to hear of the school's latest endeavour. The children have been asked to knit squares for blankets. They will be sponsored at so much per square, and the completed blankets will be donated to appropriate charities.

Although the motivation behind these letters lies in the information they share or solicit, remember that there is an added bonus when the publication where they appear sends payment for their use.

Humorous Anecdotes

Humour in writing is always popular, and if your letter raises a smile it has a good chance of acceptance.

Remember that a tale told against yourself is funny. A tale which makes someone else look silly is embarrassing. This is a true experience:

We were having a meal with some friends, and finished it with apple and blackberry turnovers hot from the oven and topped with ice cream. I thought they tasted rather peculiar, but carried on eating out of politeness. Imagine our hostess's embarrassment when she discovered a piece of carrot in hers. Those 'fruit turnovers' were really Cornish pasties taken from the wrong package in the freezer.

The occasion described ended in a lot of laughter, but in this format it makes the reader feel uncomfortable. Using poetic licence, it can be turned into an acceptable anecdotal letter:

We were entertaining some friends to a meal, and finished it with apple and blackberry turnovers hot from the oven and topped with ice cream. I thought mine tasted rather peculiar, and noticed that the guests were continuing to eat politely but had gone very quiet. Imagine my embarrassment when I bit into a piece of carrot. Those 'fruit turnovers' were really Cornish pasties taken from the wrong package in the freezer.

21

The best humorous anecdotes are rooted in truth, even if some liberties have been taken as in this example. Your own fund of these will be limited to your experience. Become a bit devious and 'borrow' funny stories from your friends. Remember, though, that your letter becomes unnecessarily convoluted if you try to explain it as 'a funny thing that happened to my cousin's next-door neighbour's brother's niece'. Fit yourself into the story, and it works.

Family Anecdotes

Every family has its own special fund of stories – the ones your mother embarrassed you with in front of a new partner, or the ones repeated *ad nauseam* when everyone has hit the sherry bottle at Christmas.

This family folklore is another good source of letters. Although the stories will have accumulated over many years, there is no need to place them in a historical context. Give them immediacy by bringing them up to date. This letter was published with my name on it as the writer:

> After a display of bad table manners, I told my daughter she was not fit to eat with the family and must take her meal to the kitchen and eat with the dog. She seemed quite happy about the situation, but the dog watched in alarm, picked up his bone and trotted off disgustedly down the path.

In fact, this was a true story, but I was the guilty party. It had happened around thirty years before the letter was published.

Confused Sayings

The suggestion was made that tales told against other people are embarrassing rather than funny. This idea can be relaxed when the very young or extremely elderly say funny things.

My late grandmother was famed for a remark which earned a place in a reader's letter:

My grandmother complained about a recipe she had been given by a neighbour. 'I've got a chart for turning gas regulo into fahrenheit,' she told us. 'But I have terrible trouble turning-fahrenheit into centimetres.' Not surprising, perhaps.

At the other end of the scale, my daughter provided me with this comment:

My husband brought our 3-year old into the hospital to see the new baby. She examined it carefully, then asked, 'If you are very good, will the nurses let you bring her home?'

It is tempting to make up confused sayings. Resist the temptation. If they are not genuine, they never quite ring true.

Tips

Any hint which makes a task run more smoothly can be counted as a tip. Most tips relate to domestic circumstances, and involve gardening, DIY, housework or cooking.

These are the shortest form of readers' letters. They involve the brief outline of an idea which will save time, solve a problem, make an economy, etc. For example:

The easiest way to 'water' a hanging basket is to throw ice cubes into it.

Or:

Put your candles in the freezer for an hour before lighting them. They will burn more slowly and more evenly.

Train yourself to come up with ideas for tips by making a conscious effort to think your way through every routine task you undertake. Keep asking yourself why you are doing things in a particular way. The answers may turn into publishable pieces of advice.

When you think of an idea for a tip, you may react by saying to yourself: 'There's nothing new in that – I've been doing it for years.' And this is often the case. You must remember, however, that the little practices you have developed over a period of time and now do as a matter of habit are clever, original ideas for people who have never thought of them.

23

Overheards

Overheard remarks make excellent readers' letters. Keep your ears flapping at all times in public places, and you will be rewarded with a collection of malapropisms and double-entendres. Sometimes the remark stands on its own, and the circumstances where you heard it are irrelevant. This conversation took place on a train.

'. . . So it came as a dreadful shock when his parents found out he was going out with other men.'
    'Yes – to look at him you'd never think he was bilingual.'

There are occasions when the location is a vital part of the letter. This conversation was overheard in the exotic lingerie department of a local store:

'What turns your husband on?'
'Two till ten.'

If the siting of the conversation were not given, there would be no humour in the remark. The double meaning, of course, depends on the reader's willingness to imagine an apostrophe in 'turn's'.

Verse

Some letters pages use poetry on a regular basis. If you enjoy writing verse and have not noticed any poems on the page of a particular magazine, it might be worth making a brief telephone call to the magazine to ask whether they would be willing to consider poetry.

Verses for these pages should be kept short, and should be rhymed and have a strict metre (or beat). As soon as a weak rhyme or oddly stressed line occurs, the poem ceases to make any impact.

Try not to make the lines in your poem too long. Consider the shape of the columns on a letters page. If long lines demand that every line of your poem needs to occupy two lines of column space, your work will be taking up an inordinate amount of room.

Verses with a twist or humorous message, or descriptive pieces are especially popular. These two have both been used on letters pages:

Middle Age

> Some may say they rue the day
> they passed the age of thirty.
> I give three cheers for middle years –
> I celebrate each birthday.
> No more high heels or diet meals
> make me a slave to fashion.
> I worry not that mole or spot
> will kill a boyfriend's passion.
> No more I'll pinch in every inch,
> make up as for the stage.
> You keep your youth –
> I've learned the truth.
> I'm loving middle age.

And in a different style:

Child Memories

> Waves cold
> Wet my feet,
> Bucket, spade,
> Picnic treat.
> Shells pale
> By my hand,
> Castles built
> In the sand.
> Lie down
> In the sun.
> Races, games –
> Years of fun!

Unlike other forms of letter, verses should be titled.

Observations

This is probably the largest category, in that it includes everything which does not find a slot elsewhere. Your observation may be original, thought-provoking, clever or wise. On the other hand, it may be trivial, flippant or downright silly. It simply needs to say enough to interest a reader of the letters page.

These two examples arose from casual reflection, and have both been published:

> I have never quite grown out of a delight in bonfires and fire-works. So why is it that every November 5th finds me cooped up in the house preparing food for hordes of hungry children, sooth-ing the cat and making gallons of coffee for the adults? I don't usually emerge until the last rocket as they are putting the fire out. Oh to be six years old again!

And:

> Now that many cars come fitted with a warning light which indi-cates whether the seat belts are fastened or not, would it be too much to hope for a 'darkness meter' to register when light condi-tions are failing? Such a device would, I am sure, prevent count-less accidents. It is all too easy to neglect the twilight conditions on a long drive, or to start the car at night and forget to switch the lights on.

The observation is another form of letter which you can usefully recount second-hand. Observations which crop up in conversation are fair game for the letter writer. Do not feel guilty about writing them up and submitting them to a magazine. After all, there is no copyright on ideas.

4

IDEAS FOR LETTERS

Sometimes it is extremely difficult to get the brain into gear and produce a batch of letters. There are a few tricks you can practise which offer good devices for kick-starting the imagination. But these will only work if you are thinking and feeling as a writer thinks and feels.

Developing the Writer's Mind

In order to function as a writer, make sure that you always view the world through a writer's eyes. One hopes that you are already establishing a notebook of ideas which never leaves you; but the ideas will not merely drop into your lap. You should seek them out wherever you can.

Make a deliberate search for the incongruous and clever. Read signs in shop windows, for example, and make a note of those which make you look twice. A double-fronted shop in a Yorkshire village had 'Do It Yourself' over the left hand window, and 'Undertaker' over the right. Inevitably it was referred to locally as the 'Do it yourself undertaker', and that fact was recorded as a reader's letter.

If you carry a camera with you, you can double your chances of selling an idea. That picture of the sign over the shop windows was worth any number of words of description.

Do not keep your eyes fixed only on the shops. Look all around you every time you go out. I once spotted an immaculate yellow car with an ugly dent in the rear wing. Someone had inscribed on it in red paint 'My wife did this'. Again, this produced a letter and a photograph, which both sold.

Look at road signs. You might be lucky enough to see something like the famous camel which found its way onto a 'Beware – animals on the road' sign in Somerset. This is a rarity, but many of the firms conducting road repairs have eyecatching and unusual signs to warn motorists of their presence.

Apply a little imagination to an ordinary road sign and you can give it a whole new slant. The sign displaying 'Cones Helpline' and giving a telephone number is not particularly interesting on its own; but imagine the cone agony aunt at the other end of the telephone, and you have material for a letter. This type of lateral thinking can be applied to signs of all sorts.

Keep an open mind when you go shopping. Look at the offers in your local supermarket. The double chocolate gateau which was accompanied by a free pot of low-fat cream substitute was a gift for a letter to a dieting magazine. The barbecue charcoal placed next to a display of sting creams and insect repellents was more a threat than an invitation, and so made a reader's letter.

Indulge in people-watching. Everyone concentrates so hard on the business of shopping that their usually hidden mannerisms appear. Watch them carefully. Look into their baskets – you're a writer, you are allowed to be nosy – and draw conclusions about their lifestyle from their purchases. There are few shopping trips which do not yield letter and filler ideas.

A simple stroll along the road will prompt letter themes. Look into people's gardens, observe the antics of any cats and dogs you see, scrutinise the passers-by. The notebook advice becomes superfluous. There is so much to see that you will not have time to write it all down.

Back home, spend a little time with the newspaper. The unfortunate juxtaposition of a photograph and a different feature, a misprint, or an unusual snippet of information are material for letters. Read the advertisements carefully. 'Car for sale, one careful lady owner with four good tyres and new exhaust' may be an old chestnut, but it still sells.

Watch the television and listen to the radio constructively. News, documentary and magazine programmes will furnish dozens of ideas when your imagination begins to flag. Take the germ of an idea from this type of source, and add your own imagination to make the resulting letter uniquely yours.

The Twenty Letters Exercise

At this stage, it would be a good idea to spend a little time creating a series of readers' letters on given themes. You will note that most of the ideas are aimed at the general interest/women's magazine market.

For each of the suggestions offered, produce a letter and send it to the appropriate outlet, being sure to keep careful records.

It might be interesting to time yourself as you work. This is not a race, of course, but it is useful to know how long it takes you to produce a good letter. Fifteen minutes from conception to postage stamp is an excellent time – but if you are new to readers' letters, do not be alarmed if it takes longer than you expect.

1 Think back to your last holiday. Did any event strike you as being funny, unexpected or particularly annoying? Condense it into a letter.

2 On the same holiday theme, have you any tips to offer about packing? Getting by in a foreign language? Making the most of a coach trip / hired car / outing?

3 Have a look at today's newspaper. Which story makes you feel most angry? Write a letter to the paper outlining the reasons for your anger.

4 Staying with the newspaper, ask yourself which story or feature made you laugh aloud. Does that story remind you of a tale from your own life? If so, you may have a good anecdotal letter for a magazine.

5 Think ahead six months. What season will it be? You might consider summer or winter, or be more specific with thoughts of the daffodil season, shooting season or Christmas. Write a letter appropriate to that season, and send it to a weekly magazine. It should be in good time for publication.

6 Recall the last time you spent an evening in congenial company. What made you laugh aloud? Recount the story as a magazine letter.

7 Turn on your radio, and make a note of the first sentence you hear. Write a letter which includes that sentence. When you have finished, alter the original sentence and you will have a fresh piece for submission.

8 Think back to your childhood. What pleasures did you enjoy that today's children seem to have missed? Ask yourself 'Whatever happened to . . .' and write a letter including your reply.

9 Remember the last occasion when you spent some time in the company of small children. Did a child say or do anything funny or remarkable? Did you have to entertain a child? If so, what did you do? The answer could be a good tip for a busy parent.

10 Recall the last time you cried, or felt like crying. Were you motivated by sadness, anger or even hilarity? Would an account of the occasion make a letter?

11 Go into your kitchen or garage. Look around you. Think carefully about the routine you would undertake to perform any task there. How would you make the task easier for yourself? The answer might be a tip.

12 Think about any local charity whose concerns are dear to your heart. Could you raise public awareness of its concerns by writing a letter to your local paper?

13 Look out of your window. Create a letter from something you see. You can repeat this exercise *ad infinitum* if 'your' window is the window of a train, a hotel, or another unfamiliar setting.

14 Watch a TV comedy. Take any of the themes that give rise to laughter, and write a brief, rhyming verse about it for a magazine letters page.

15 Visit a local place of interest – a stately home, zoo, picturesque walk, etc. Create a letter out of anything you find there.

16 Examine your most treasured possession. Is there a story attached to it?

17 Do you have a pet? If so, is there a funny tale you can tell? If not, do you know somebody with a dog/cat/gerbil with a good story?

18 Write an account of your ideal way of spending an evening out, or a day off. Submit it to a magazine, closing your letter with a question along the lines of: 'How do other readers make the most of their leisure time?'

19 Look carefully through all your family photographs. Does one of them have a special story associated with it? Submit

- A letter railing against children who can never hand over notes given to them by teachers/Brownie leaders only moments before.
- An expression of annoyance that one may be able to produce masterpieces in the kitchen when no one but the family will ever see them, but that when the offerings are destined for other people, everything goes wrong.
- A complaint about the time-consuming demands made by various organisations on busy Mums, when a straightforward donation would be so much easier to arrange.
- A tongue-in-cheek tip explaining that lemon cheese is the most appropriately glutinous medium for welding together a broken sandwich cake, and that hundreds-and-thousands can hide a multitude of sins in terms of scuffed icing.
- An anecdotal letter describing the handing-in of the 'disaster' cake and the purchasing of the wrong cake.

Over a few months, each of these five letters was accepted, and the payments I received totalled considerably more than my regular fee from the article outlet.

There is a postscript to this story. While I was analysing the piece to divide it into letters, I spent some time reading passages of it aloud. (This is always a good idea, to check that a piece of writing flows smoothly.) It occurred to me that I had a suitable piece for radio transmission, and my local station took the full article and made their usual small payment for its use. About a year after the original rejection, a new editor took over the care of my regular slot. I resubmitted 'The Brownie Cake' in its entirety, and it was published.

This is not intended as an exercise in smugness. It is an object lesson in never throwing anything away. Not only can material originally intended for a longer treatment be diverted into readers' letters, but a change of staff may mean a change of fortune. All you need is patience and belief in your piece of writing. If it bounces back too frequently, you will know that your faith was misplaced.

Photographs

The suggestion has already been made that it is a good idea to keep a camera with you. You do not need to be an expert photographer to take acceptable snaps. You are aiming to produce a picture with clear definition, uncluttered so that the point of the picture is obvious.

An ordinary, basic camera is perfectly adequate. After all, you are not aiming to take glamour shots or breathtaking landscapes. You are simply looking for an interesting picture.

Many letter pages have a special slot for a photograph with a witty caption. In most cases, they will reproduce your picture from an ordinary colour print.

Pictures of children and animals are especially sought after. As any actor will tell you, these are not the ideal subjects. Unless you are highly proficient with a camera, good photographs of these subjects have an element of luck involved. Be prepared to take plenty of pictures in the hope that one or two will prove saleable.

A picture which is unusual or specially interesting is worth keeping on file until you can think of a really clever caption to go with it. A series of pictures telling their own story has instant appeal.

When you are submitting pictures, be sure to put your name and address onto the back of each one. Do not use ballpoint pen, which could damage the photograph. Use a pencil, or invest in pre-printed stickers.

To prevent creases in your pictures, you can buy envelopes stiffened with card, or simply cut a piece of cardboard slightly larger than your pictures and use it for support. If you want your photographs to be returned, be sure to send a similarly strengthened s.a.e. for this purpose.

Do not send your negatives, or the only copy of a prized photograph. Although the utmost care will be taken with your pictures in the editorial office, human error or postal problems can result in the loss of a picture. (For the same reason, keep a copy of every piece of writing, however short, which goes out of your house.)

If you are bitten by the photography bug and, as a writer, want to make further use of your camera, consult the excellent 'Photography for Article-Writers' by Gordon Wells (Allison and Busby).

5

FILLERS

There is a grey area where the material for fillers overlaps that used in readers' letters. In many cases, the only difference between a letter and a filler is in its presentation and the fact that it is not directed in the address to a specific page. The letter page is beautifully signposted; all letters are gathered together under a headline which indicates clearly that these are readers' contributions. But it is possible for filler opportunities to go unrecognised.

Fillers, by their nature, occupy little slots of space which enhance the look of a page. A large chunk of print, perhaps a page of a short story, is broken up with a boxed snippet; or a filler occupies an inch or two at the bottom of a column.

Even though modern computer techniques have solved the old typesetter's problem of leaving blocks of blank space on the page – the ideal spot for placing a filler – fillers are still popular. Editors appreciate the busy feel they give to a piece of otherwise uninterrupted text.

Anecdotes, tips, confused sayings, misprints and observations could all appear either as letters or as fillers. The following additional topics can also create fillers:

Quotations

If you have ever browsed through a dictionary of quotations, you will know how fascinating it is to survey the pithy thoughts of past generations.

A quotation can be submitted as a one-off. If you come across an unusual or humorous saying, send it away on its own with a note of its originator's name and dates.

It is more interesting, perhaps, to send a short series of quotations. Put them into a logical grouping. They may all have been originated by the same person, or by people who lived at the same time.

It is fascinating to collect quotations on a set subject. Make a collection of the pronouncements of the famous on the monarchy, travel, contemporary art of the day, writing, love, etc. Put half a dozen together and submit them as a block. Do not become carried away, and send every piece of material you have on your chosen subject. Keep something in reserve to send on a future occasion.

If you are quoting from written material, make sure that the writers have been dead for at least seventy years in order to avoid copyright complications.

Jokes

A successful joke is unlikely to bring fame to its writer. The writer is forgotten, and the joke filters through all sections of society, being altered and expanded *en route*.

When producing a joke as a filler, do not try to create a prolonged 'shaggy dog' story. Keep it crisp and punchy, or the reader will lose interest before getting to the end of your tale.

Even for those writers with an excellent sense of humour, creating an original joke is difficult. One approach is to take any joke you have heard, analyse its humour, and then attempt to reproduce that style of humour using your original joke as a template.

For example, you might start with the simple, direct original:

What lies at the bottom of the sea and shivers? A nervous wreck.

This depends on an immediately recognised phrase which has a double meaning. To create your own joke in this form, it would be a good idea to start with the recognisable phrase in the same grammatical format as the original, eg. a red herring, a trifling problem, a sorry mess. Now analyse the phrase for any alternative meanings, and come up with an appropriate question:

What's too embarrassed to give you a clue?
A red herring.

What sits in a bowl of custard feeling depressed?
A trifling problem.

What keeps apologising for staining the carpet?
A sorry mess.

As this example demonstrates, you are unlikely to come up with a joke every time you apply the technique; but the more you try, the more easily the ideas will flow. Somewhere along the line you will encounter an original thought which is even funnier than your traditional, starter joke.

The same analysis technique can be applied to any form of joke, for example:

Doctor, doctor, people keep ignoring me.
Next!

The humour here derives from a link between the patient's problem and the doctor's apparently uncaring reply. Think up a new problem:

Doctor, doctor, I feel as if my leg's dropping off.
Hop it.

Again, the more ideas you come up with at a sitting, the better they are likely to become.

Many jokes depend on making stereotyped assumptions about a group of people, eg. mothers-in-law or people from a particular country. They depend on laughing at people's problems, such as deafness or age, on mocking religion, or on highlighting anything connected with sex.

Jokes may be as mild and childish as the examples given above, or mordantly satirical. In jokes we try to debunk anything that worries or frightens us by laughing at it.

Every writer of jokes must decide on the style and level of humour which is right and comfortable for that individual. If you are going to send a joke to 'The Weekly News', you will not use the same material you would create if writing for a blue comedian's stage show.

Palindromes

Words, phrases and dates which read the same backwards and forwards are fascinating. By setting a few examples and asking readers to offer their favourites, you can create an interesting filler. The most famous is probably the one dedicated to Napoleon:

Able was I ere I saw Elba.

Try to think of a series of palindromes within a given category, eg. women's names:

Eve, Ava, Ada, Lil, Anna, Madam.

Find a linking factor to connect palindromic dates. This does not need to be as difficult as it sounds. You can even do this with years, without taking days and months into account. Is there any factor which 1661, 1771, 1881 and 1991 had in common?

Even if there is no common factor, you could make an interesting filler simply by listing a notable event for each of these specially numbered years.

Playing With Words

Writers are fascinated by words, so it should not be too arduous a task to come up with a few ideas for puns or word play which could be grouped together into fillers.

For example, a perennial favourite is the fictitious book title and author:

Arboriculture	by Teresa Green.
Problems in Banking	by Noah Count.
Scrap Metal Recycling	by N. E. Oldiron.
Motor Mechanics for Ladies	by Wilma Carstart.

and to avoid any accusations of sexism –

Can Your Man Cook?	by Betty Carnt.

The same general principle can be applied to other ideas, of course. Think of the right person for the job:

For plumbing needs, contact Ivor Plunger.
Speedy-stitch wedding dresses by Marion Saturday.
Off-licence proprietress – Jean Antonick.

Take a familiar saying and find a new way to finish it:

Many hands make a bonanza for glove manufacturers.
A stitch in time saves a lot of embarrassment.
Take care of the pennies and you'll be labelled a tightfisted so-and-so.

A series of these would make a filler. You can do the same thing with familiar verses, and you do not need to worry about retaining the rhyme:

Mary, Mary, quite contrary, how does your garden grow? With silver bells and cockle shells and the biggest load of manure you never wanted to see.

Humpty Dumpty sat on a wall, Humpty Dumpty had a great fall, All the King's horses and all the King's men said, 'Hang on, the Prime Minister's visit isn't till next week, save the egg throwing till then.'

You can create a filler simply by defining words in the idiom of a particular group of people. For the comments made after a reading at a writers' circle, you might use these definitions:

intriguing	—	I didn't understand much of it.
deep	—	I didn't understand any of it.
multi-layered	—	I didn't understand, but maybe I should pretend to.
surreal	—	nobody understands a syllable.

You would use an entirely different set of words and definitions if your target was a group of estate agents:

homely	— needs decorating.
quaint	— needs new plumbing.
picturesque gardens	— hire a rotovator.
partial central heating	— not all the radiators work.
planning permission available	— hire the demolition crew.

Anagrams have their own fascination. Make a list of the names of a set of people (politicians, for example, or US presidents) or play titles, etc., and see whether you can produce anagrams of them:

Hamlet	—	halt me.
Romeo and Juliet	—	joiner to laud me.
The Tempest	—	tempt sheet.

If the anagrams happen to make appropriate words or phrases, so much the better.

Channel your thoughts into word usages, and you will find all sorts of original ideas for fillers.

Series of Facts

Most of the filler ideas suggested so far have been flippant ones. You can make a fascinating filler by grouping together a list of interesting facts about a subject. This is likely to have a slightly more serious line of approach.

Find half a dozen things the average person might not be expected to know about water recycling, the life of Disraeli, tramcars, Bolivia – any subject under the sun. String the facts together with brief linking passages, or merely list them, and you have a filler. For example:

> Have you ever watched a hot air balloon gliding gracefully over the countryside? Did you realise that its pilot has to pass the same examinations as an airline pilot? A balloon travels at the same speed as the wind. Thermal currents make early morning and late afternoon the most appropriate times for balloon trips. From a balloon, passengers can see a stripe in the atmosphere, where the pollution below meets the clean air above. Balloons rotate slowly and of their own accord while in the air.

You are aiming to make the reader think 'I never knew that', and perhaps to fascinate him into wanting to discover more about your chosen subject.

The easiest way to accumulate facts for these fillers is to keep everything you can find about as many topics as you can. A simple card index box with alphabetical file cards will hold all your snippets of information. When you want to produce a filler, draw out the notes and the newspaper and magazine cuttings you have collected relating to the topic of your choice.

You are not necessarily going to use all your information in one go. Again, keep something back for your next filler on the same subject.

Remember that there is no copyright on facts; only on the actual wording of your original information. For example, you might have a piece of information which states:

> In the 1920s there were over 14,000 tramcars in the U.K. These brought a new mobility to the working man, who no longer had to work within walking distance of his home.

You could be infringing copyright if you wrote those words in that order in a filler piece about tramcars. All you need to do is alter the format, eg:

> The 14,000 tramcars in use in Britain during the 1920s gave the working man more choice in where he lived. It was no longer necessary for him to live close to his workplace.

These factual fillers will find homes in a range of magazines and newspapers, and may also be appropriate for the publications associated with a particular occupation.

Trade papers frequently accept freelance contributions. If you have a good idea for a factual filler on the grocery trade, social work, teaching, etc., approach the relevant trade press outlet with your submission.

Children's Fillers

When you are considering writing fillers, do not forget that these snippets are enjoyed by children just as much as by adults. They are used in children's comics, and also on specially designated children's pages in adults' newspapers and magazines.

The subject headings considered above are just the same for the younger reader, but of course your material should be selected with the outlet's target age range firmly in mind.

If you do not have any contact with children, or are unsure of the subjects and levels of understanding appropriate to particular ages, check your ideas with a teacher who knows that age group.

Approach the editor of your chosen page with some examples of your writing for children and, if possible, other ideas on which you would like to work.

If your local newspaper does not have a page for children, why not suggest one? You would be in at the start as a contributor to the page, and who knows, you might even end up with a commission to put the whole page together!

Presentation of Fillers

It is usual to submit fillers a few at a time. Send a very brief covering letter, and offer each filler on a separate sheet of paper which bears your name, address and telephone number.

Your fillers should be typed double spaced, using one side only of a sheet of A4 paper. Leave wide margins all around your work.

As ever, be sure to send an s.a.e. if you expect a reply from the editor. (This is the standard procedure for manuscript presentation.)

Supplying Facts

There are some outlets which will make fillers or even complete articles from facts supplied by freelance writers. If a publication follows this practice, there will be a note, usually affixed to an article which has been written in this way, saying something like:

> Do you have an interesting story to tell? Have you ever been through an experience similar to the one described here? Our readers would like to hear about it. Send brief details on a post-card, and our reporter will contact you. We will pay £x for every story we use. If a publication does not solicit material in this way, you are unlikely to be paid for submitting an idea for an article. You may, of course, get a commission to write a piece, but your idea could be taken up and written in-house. (There is no copyright on ideas.)

Short Solicited Pieces

Many magazines have a column which is regularly filled with a short-short article on a recurring theme. The editor may ask writers to submit an account of their idea of a perfect day, or to describe something they find irritating. The subject could be the place where you live, or a favourite possession.

To write for such a column, you will need to apply the same skills you require for readers' letters. You have a tightly limited wordage, and you must be sure not to exceed this. Keep to the point, and use an informal, chatty style just as you would in a letter.

Write as if you were speaking. Pretend you are going to chat with an acquaintance about the topic of the piece, and share information in an open, friendly manner.

Make sure that you indicate clearly the column for which your work is intended. Add a coversheet to your manuscript which bears your name, address and telephone number, your title, wordage (to the nearest 50 words, say) and the destination of your writing. For example:

'24 Hours in Paris' — a feature of 200 words for consideration for the 'My Favourite Day' column.

Many of these columns appear on a magazine's letters page, but others will be scattered through the publication. Read carefully to make sure you do not miss the opportunity of a sale.

Check specialist magazines thoroughly for these solicited articles. There are many spaces for readers' experiences in the sphere of interest covered by the magazine. One point to note: if photographs are required, check the form of presentation preferred by telephoning the magazine. Although most general interest magazines can use ordinary colour prints, some specialist magazines insist on monochrome prints or transparencies.

6

ULTRA-SHORT FICTION

It is more difficult to place fiction than non-fiction. Ultra-short fiction, which for our purposes is defined as fiction in 500 words or less, has few outlets. It is still a topic worth considering, for four reasons.

First, there are some occasions – albeit rare – when commercial outlets are seeking extremely short fiction, or when it is the subject of a competition.

Secondly, the experience of writing in any form is never a waste of time. Every piece you write, whether or not it produces a saleable item, adds to your stock of creative achievements.

Thirdly, writing very short fiction is relaxing and pleasurable. It is easy to lose sight of the sheer fun of writing, and a shame when this happens. You will keep your style lively and interesting by remaining interested in your own work, and by enjoying the process of its creation.

Finally, by remaining alert to the sales potential of everything you produce, you may realise that there is an unexpected outlet for some longer version of your ultra-short writing.

The Mini-Saga

The mini-saga only emerged as a recognised writing form in the last quarter of the twentieth century. It is therefore so new that it has not had time to win popularity. It could be that authors of the future will produce this form of writing for collections of mini-sagas which will become bestsellers.

At the time of preparing this book, the major outlet for mini-sagas is the occasional competition featuring them. The way has been paved for published collections, however, as compilations of successful competition entries have appeared in print.

A mini-saga is a story complete in itself and told in fifty words precisely – not forty-nine, not fifty-one. There is not, as yet, any consensus on the use of words with hyphens. In the absence of information and remembering the precision required in the word-count, it is a good idea to avoid hyphenated words. It may have a title, which can be of any length up to fifteen words.

The story should have a beginning, a middle and an end, and its narration should move naturally to a conclusion which pleases, puzzles or fascinates. It should use normal grammar and sentence construction.

It may be simple and lighthearted. For example:

THE AWAKENING OF ETHEL WINTERBOTTOM

Ethel Winterbottom knew there was more to life than censoring the Enid Blytons. Then the librarians were invited to a mayoral reception. Indifferent sherry made her head reel. She was taken home in the mayor's car, where a drunken councillor slipped his hand up her thigh. So this was living.

It can deal with huge, complex topics in its brief confines:

LOOKING AFTER

Marianne was fifteen when they took her baby's life away. They told her she could never look after a child. The incinerator would look after it. Years later she wanted more babies, but their eyes haunted her nights, tortured her days. Marianne was fifteen when they took her life away.

There are two special bonuses for the writer of mini-sagas. One is that a completed mini-saga may give you the notes for a full-length short story. The other is that, with a little alteration and the addition of alignment, a mini-saga can be converted into a free verse poem. Consider this:

PEA CHANGE

Fascination started with an ornament, gaudy peacock memento. Pictures came next – postcards of peacocks, each question mark of neck fleshing into plump body, burgeoning to proudly iridescent tail. Her room exuded peacock presence. Unsurprised, she felt brown feathers downing her body, thrust of wings, bloom of response peahenning within her.

With only the slightest changes, it becomes:

PEA CHANGE

Fascination started
with an ornament,
gaudy peacock memento.

Pictures came next –
postcards of peacocks,
each question mark of neck
fleshing into plump body,
burgeoning proud to iridescent tail.
Her room exuded peacock presence.

Unsurprised, she felt
brown feathers downing her body,
thrust of wings,
bloom of response peahenning within.

Whenever you write a mini-saga, you gain the invaluable experience of honing your skills of conciseness and precision in the use of language – vital to every writer. By expanding the mini-saga into a poem or short story, you are immediately creating a potentially saleable piece of writing.

Debased Stories

This technique has no commercial application, unless, perhaps, you could persuade a magazine to take such a story as a filler. It is fun to do, and entertaining to share.

The idea is to take any familiar story, and debase it by changing the ending. Here is a simple example:

Snow White was a beautiful princess whose wicked stepmother tried to kill her with a poisoned apple. She hid in the home of seven dwarves, who forced her to do all the housework and never let her go out. Her stepmother gave the dodgy apple to her elderly husband, let Snow White's room to a handsome prince, and the two of them lived happily ever after and kept an orchard.

As with the mini-saga, this is not necessarily a piece of writing produced just for its own sake. A short story or poem based on the debased story can be submitted and sold.

Ultra-Short Stories

Some magazines feature a bona fide short story of under 500 words. These are probably the most difficult stories to write.

Your task in writing one is to offer your reader a complete and interesting piece which can be digested in just a couple of minutes. There should be a plot, absorbing character/s, conflict, atmosphere, dialogue, background – in fact, all the elements which combine to create a full short story.

There is no room for a wasted syllable. Every word you put down has to contribute its full worth to the story, adding to the reader's understanding of the whole.

As with non-fiction shorts, the more of these you attempt, the more easily the technique will come to you. If you can write acceptable stories to this length, you have the chance of finding yourself a comfortable niche in the market. This is a highly specialised skill, and not a universal accomplishment.

For further information, consult Stella Whitelaw's extremely helpful volume, 'How to Write Short-short Stories' (Allison and Busby).

Monologues

There is a small market for published monologues of a maximum 500 words, and tremendous interest in such pieces for use in concerts and as party entertainment.

The monologue is a dramatic piece for a single speaker, who may be addressing the audience directly, talking into a telephone, or speaking to an invisible stage presence. (The classic longer monologues performed by Joyce Grenfell made the audience assume the presence of a nursery school class being addressed by the teacher.)

The narrator must have something to say. It may be poignant, witty, tragic or farcical, but it must be worth hearing. A monologue on the subject of the price of fish would be incredibly boring, unless it was delivered by somebody who could not afford the fish; or by a dizzy character who included the information in a string of domestic misadventures; or by the widow of a fisherman who had drowned.

Monologues must be conversational. You should be able to imagine they are being delivered over the garden fence or standing at the bar. At the risk of sounding repetitive, like all shorts they do not allow any scope for waffle. Every word must count.

Short Fiction Exercises

Even though fiction is notoriously difficult to place, it is worth spending a little time practising the skills of fiction-writing in the form of exercises. They will enhance your powers of observation, and assist you in perfecting the techniques of expressing yourself concisely and effectively. This will benefit all the writing you undertake, in whatever style.

While you are working through these exercises, keep your mind alert to the idea of developing them into saleable pieces of writing.

Allow a maximum of ten minutes for each, and tackle no more than three or four at a sitting, or they will become tedious:

1 Write a character study of a real person you admire, living or dead, either known to you or a celebrity. Keep within the bounds of truth as you know or understand it. Now add a whopping fictional flaw to the individual's character.

2 Using the character study you prepared in Exercise 1, give the character a problem compatible with his/her nature, and a possible route for solving the problem. Make the character flaw significant, by having it contribute in some way to the problem or the solution.

3 Think of a scene you can recall from any book you have enjoyed reading. Now place that scene in a different location of your own devising. Either write a straightforward description of the location, or write a version of the scene in your own words using your new background.

4 Produce a mini-saga which explores the relationship between any two characters.

5 Using your imagination as well as experience or knowledge, give 150-word descriptions of some establishment as it was a century ago, as it is today, and as it will be a hundred years from now. You might choose a house, a hospital, a church, a bar etc.

6 Using the same techniques, write descriptions of some aspect of the countryside in the past, present and future. (This will probably be more difficult.)

7 Write a 100-word précis of the perfect crime. (If you are pleased with it, you could perhaps flesh it out to make a complete story.)

8 Take some brief anecdote from your childhood. Write about it in the third person, ascribing your own memories and experiences to somebody else.

9 Write the notes for an ultra-short story which has a beginning, a middle and an end.

10 Open any novel, and copy down the first sentence of the book. Without reading any further, continue to produce the opening paragraph of a story of your devising. When you have done so, look back at the original. Are there any similarities? Which opening paragraph would tempt you to read the rest of the story?

11 Create a brief circular story (in no more than 200 words) –

one, in other words, where the last sentence is the same as the first, and the reader has come, nightmare fashion, back to the beginning. (This exercise may provide you with the idea for a poem.)

12 Write a few lines of dialogue between two characters, one being a figure of authority, the other in a subordinate position.

13 Make a character sketch of the individual you would choose to narrate a monologue, and give the character a problem to be treated in the monologue.

14 Write a paragraph of about 100 words taken from any point in a story, featuring a natural item such as rock, water, a fossil etc. If the result pleases you, you could go on to write the whole story.

15 Think about any story you like – a true family anecdote, a novel, a plotline in a soap opera etc. You will automatically associate it with one individual's viewpoint. Write a version of the story in no more than 200 words, looking at the events through a different character's eyes.

16 Convert the material from any anecdotal reader's letter you have produced in the past into a mini-saga.

17 Select a word at random by sticking a pin in the dictionary. Write the first three sentences of a story, using the same word to open each.

18 Take any bible story or traditional fairy tale and write an updated version of it in 150 words. Once more, you could have produced the notes that can be written up in the form of a poem.

19 Write 150 words of any story where every verb is qualified by an adverb. Go back through the story deleting the adverbs and changing the verbs so that they express the original meaning most completely.

20 In 100 words create a character, give him/her a problem, a location, an advantage, a disadvantage and another character. (These could be the notes for a full-length short story.)

One of the beauties of these exercises is that they start the creative juices flowing. This is very useful if you are warming up to producing a longer piece of work. As well as this, they provide you with an additional example of writing which can be expanded in order to make it suitable for selling.

Remain open to the possibilities of other ideas cropping up while you are working through an exercise. If such an idea occurs to you, be sure to make notes immediately, before you have a chance to forget it. Jot down the essence of the idea, and the market for which you will develop it.

The broader your options for further writing, the better. Do not feel restricted to writing to a particular length simply because this book is concentrating on shorts. Allow yourself the scope to create full-length articles, stories or even books – or at least to produce the detailed notes which might grow into any of these.

7

POETRY

Apart from the readers' letters pages, which have already been considered, there are many more outlets for writers to use short verse. Most of these outlets prefer poetry in traditional patterns rather than free verse. Whatever your selected market, you will stand the greatest chance of success if you keep to these guidelines.

- Make sure that your poem has something original to say, and says it effectively
- Stay within a tightly controlled subject area. Poems are too short to allow you to explore a range of topics, or to do justice to a vast subject. A poem which examines in precise terms the perfection of a bluebell will be far more effective than one which waffles in abstractions about the beauties of the countryside generally.
- No matter which pattern of poetry you choose to convey your message, stay with the same form throughout the poem. For example, if your first stanza has alternate lines rhyming, do not change the pattern to have consecutive lines rhyming in the second.
- Use rhyme with precision, but make its application appear effortless. Do not wrench sense or meaning for the sake of placing a rhyming word at the end of a line. Seek out the word that fits. If nothing appropriate rhymes with your key sound, alter the whole poem to produce a new key sound which rhymes with the word you need.
- Write in today's language and idiom. Contractions such as 'ne'er' for 'never' and archaic words like 'oft' and 'ere' are no longer acceptable.

- Avoid grammatical constructions you would never dream of using in conversation, such as 'we do go a-strolling' when contemporary language demands 'we go strolling' or 'we stroll'.
- Metre is just as important as rhyme. The beat of your poem must have a regular pattern of stresses if the sound is to make sense. Speak your work aloud to ensure that the metre is harmonious throughout. Better still, speak it into a tape recorder and then listen back, or get somebody to read it out to you.

There is one important point to note about sending poetry for publication. For some unaccountable reason, there are writers who think it is appropriate to submit poetry in a less professional manner than other manuscripts. Writers who would not dream of sending in a handwritten short story or article think it is acceptable for poetry.

Indeed, poems arrive on sheets from an ordinary writing pad, written by hand on pastel-tinted paper, and even adorned with sketches, photographs or illustrations cut from magazines. Writers who use word processors are not immune to the syndrome. Fancy scripts with curls and wiggles set in boxes, or with each line centralised and the poem presented in an oval frame, will not endear the work to an editor.

Submit each poem on its own sheet of A4 paper, even if it is only a few lines long. It should be typed, but you should use a single spaced format. (Poetry is the only form of writing which should be presented in single spacing.) Allow a wide margin and start a couple of spaces down the page, so that your poem is not squashed up in the top left hand corner.

Put your name, address and telephone number on every poem. If you are submitting more than one at a time to an outlet, the pages could easily become detached. If they are not all labelled your identity as author could vanish without trace.

Keep your covering letter brief, saying no more than:

I enclose four verses which I hope you will kindly consider for publication in *The Kiddies' Christmas Verse Book*, and the usual s.a.e.

Do not forget the promised s.a.e. if you expect to receive a reply.

The Poet's Corner Slot

Some magazines have a regular Poet's Corner feature which provides a pleasing outlet for poetry, usually concentrating on short, rhymed, light verse. Read the column over a number of issues until you have absorbed the style and presentation of the feature. Check the submission requirements. You may be asked to supply a photograph, facts about yourself or comments about your interest in poetry. This information will be condensed into a tiny introduction. Keep it brief, and stay within the remit the editor requires.

Unless you are specifically asked to submit a selection of work, just send one poem at a time to a poet's corner feature.

If a publication does not feature poetry in a regular column, why not make an approach and ask whether it could be considered? It might be that the editor hates poetry and refuses to publish any, but it could be that nobody had thought of it before. A telephone call or a brief letter to ask about the omission will suffice.

Your local paper may be interested in initiating a poetry column where all the contributors are residents of your town. They might be willing to start the process by running a competition for local writers, printing an entry to the competition in each issue over a period of time, and offering small prizes for the best work.

But your best chance of initiating a special niche for poetry may be in the field of specialist magazines. The editor of a magazine about skiing or caravanning might be delighted to include an occasional poem on the subject covered by the publication. By making the offer in the first place, you are putting yourself into a most favourable position for gaining an acceptance.

Greetings Cards

If you would like to write verses for greetings cards, the best starting point is to study the market. Look at the range of cards and decide which of their messages you could have produced. A call or letter to the company publishing those cards will indicate whether they are open to freelance contributions.

While you are making this enquiry, check whether you are expected to provide the cover greeting as well as the internal message for a card.

When you are writing your own messages, note the length of verse preferred within a style of card, or the maximum and minimum number of lines in cards produced by your target outlet. Look at the length of the lines, and their rhyming pattern. If every example you study uses verses which rhyme in alternate lines, do not construct a verse which has groups of three lines rhyming together.

Having done your market study, be aware of the tone of your target publisher. Some cards are unashamedly sentimental. Others have simple, down-to-earth messages. Some look for flowery language, others for a more conversational approach. Match your tone to that of the other cards in the range.

It is difficult to strike an original note in greetings cards, because the key words used in them have appeared so frequently. If you manage to find a new message or an original way of conveying a traditional one, you have done well.

Try to make the messages in your cards as open as you can. For example, these simple words of greeting impose restrictions on the people sending the cards:

I wish you a happy birthday.

We both wish you a happy birthday.

We all wish you a happy birthday.

A universal message would be:

Wishing you a happy birthday.

Also consider the recipient:

Loving thoughts to our friends across the miles

or:

Loving thoughts to our family across the miles

would not be as acceptable as simply saying:

Loving thoughts across the miles.

There are some cases when it is essential to clarify a relationship, eg. an anniversary card from one partner to another. Under these circumstances, the more personal your message the better.

When you produce a verse for a card, you are undertaking to express the sender's feelings which he/she finds difficult to put into words. Your watchword should be sincerity. Write with fidelity to the occasion and the relationship you have in mind, and your message will be convincing.

Remember that not all greetings cards use rhyme in their messages. Some have a single phrase or sentence, while others are mere vehicles for jokes – often at the expense of the recipient. Explore the various kinds of message, always submitting your material to a card publisher who uses the style you are trying to place.

You will not make a fortune by writing greetings. Payment is usually a one-off fee, for which the publisher is entitled to use your greeting as many times as he wants. But you will also earn the satisfaction of knowing that your words are helping hundreds (if not thousands) of people to put their personal message across.

Novelty Outlets

When considering writing verse for greetings cards, think of all the associated items sold alongside cards which could carry poems.

Messages are printed on T-shirts and mugs, on posters and bookmarks. They appear on bumper stickers, notebooks, balloons, even badges, pencils and keyrings. Somebody has thought up the wording to be printed in all these places, and has been paid for producing it.

If you can think of a pithy verse which could be used by any of these outlets, why not try moving into the novelty market? Brevity is vital, and your message must punch itself across in a direct and instantly recognisable fashion.

Take the usual advice for seeking a new outlet. Look at the range of products on the market and decide which would be the best vehicle for your verse. Contact the manufacturer by concise letter or over the telephone, and ask whether your material might be of interest.

Verse Postcards

This is not a commercial outlet, but it is a pleasing exercise to undertake and one which will draw attention to your persona as a writer.

The idea is to have your own poetry printed on postcards. Your poem appears on the blank side of a plain card. The other side is then divided down the middle, for your notes to be written on the left and the address on the right, just as if you were using a picture postcard. Each time you use one to send a brief message, you are publicising yourself and your work.

If you plan to have the postcard printed portrait-angled, your chosen poem should be no more than twenty lines long, and the lines should be fairly short. If you prefer a landscape-angled presentation, go for a poem of no more than ten lines, but the lines can be quite long.

As you will not be dealing with a professional publisher but publishing it yourself, you must make extra sure that your work reaches an appropriate standard. There is no editor to reject your poetry. Produce your favourite piece of verse which you know is not exactly right, but you still like it, and you will embarrass the recipient and yourself every time you send a copy out.

If there is someone whose opinion you can trust – preferably another writer rather than a non-writing friend or relative – seek their honest advice about the quality of your work.

When you have selected a good poem which could be enjoyed

by anyone who reads it, find a printer who will produce your cards. Do not pick the first one you find. Printers' estimates are notorious for their disparity. Check half a dozen, ensuring that they are quoting for reproduction on the same quality of card. (It is a false economy to use thin card – go for the best the printer can offer.)

You may decide to have a range of poems printed on cards, but remember that it is likely to cost rather more if you use several poems than if you have the same one printed on a large number of postcards.

You can take this personal publicity verse a stage further by having the shortest verses printed on your notepaper or business cards.

Calendars and Diaries

Although the market is very limited, there is scope for short pieces of verse to be included in these publications. Desk calendars of the type where you tear off a page each day often have a funny or thought-provoking phrase written on each leaf. Rhyming couplets have particular appeal.

The verse should make an observation for its reader to carry through the day. It should be upbeat, quirky or uplifting rather than depressing. Remember that you are responsible for setting the tone of the reader's day. The more positive it is, the happier its reader.

Calendars which show a month to each page – and feature poetry – will take longer work. Again, be sure that your message is pleasant and will enrich its reader.

There are all sorts of diaries on the market, from the flimsy leaflet to the A4 page-a-day kind. Some of these feature the same type of verse as the tear-off calendars. Others print a complete verse at the beginning of each month.

Those diaries which are dedicated to readers of a publication, or to people pursuing a special interest, are a potential market. They offer scope for verses written about their particular concern, which add pleasing variety to the bulk of information included before the diary pages.

Privately-Commissioned Verse

This has nothing to do with commercial publication of poetry, but you can sell your verse on a personal level. You do this by writing a poem to fit a special occasion. For example, you might write a piece to be read at someone's leaving party, or at a social event such as a birthday or wedding.

This sort of writing is often produced by somebody's friend for the occasion in question. If you can establish a reputation for writing poetry of excellent quality, people will pay for your services.

The secret is to learn as much as you can about the subject of the poem. Discover the facts, and add all the little intimate details you can find which will reassure the subject that you have written just for them.

In this style of writing, be as personal as you can, bearing in mind, however, that the poem may be read out on a public occasion. Sometimes the gossip you learn from friends is unsuitable for general consumption, and the best bits have to be left out. Make sure that your subject receives a copy of the poem to keep.

As you will not be negotiating fees with an editor, you will have to set your own rate for your work. Decide how long it will take you to write the poem, and work out your costs for presentation. Select an hourly rate which reflects good use of your time. If you have no idea how to pitch the charge, use the current hourly rates for nightschool teachers as a yardstick.

Be realistic in both directions. If your service is too expensive, there will be few takers. If it is too cheap, you will be providing sweated labour, with no one to blame for it but yourself.

This presupposes that you will just be passing on a copy of the poem you have produced. If you wish to go in for a more elaborate presentation of your work you might have it delivered with flowers or champagne, or send a speaker to the occasion for which it was written. The speaker will halt the proceedings and declaim the poem. Remember to add realistic charges for such extras.

Depending on how heavily you want to go into this type of writing, you may just spread the word around that you are willing to undertake commissions, or conduct an advertising campaign locally, perhaps even leaving your business cards (inscribed with suitable verse, of course) at every conceivable outlet. Your pin-money writing could grow into a small business.

Verse for Children

Do not neglect the youngest readers when you are writing poetry. Children love poems with a strong rhythm and clever rhymes. Even the smallest can join in with actions associated with verse. Toddlers who cannot construct a sentence can chant nursery rhymes, or show you the actions to 'Miss Polly had a Dolly'.

Keep your vocabulary direct, but be sure you do not talk down to the child. Write about every topic under the sun, looking at children's life and daily routine, and exploring the world way beyond their experience. Even the shortest verses can have educational qualities, as well as bringing pleasure. Do not ignore the child's interest in fantasy.

Use humour for extra appeal. The same humour which appeals to adults will engage the imagination of children. Be irreverent, casting a wry sidelong glance at the adult world. Be witty, silly or zany. Be ever-so-slightly rude, remembering that a word like 'knickers' sends the average nine-year-old into paroxysms of laughter.

You may be able to sell your verse to anthologies. (Children's publishers will advise you of current projects and refer you to the editor.) Outlets for one-off poems include comics, greetings cards and the annual volumes produced shortly before Christmas. (These are allied to children's interests, television shows and publications.) Also try your work on dedicated children's pages in newspapers and magazines.

Both comics and women's magazines feature occasional stories told in verse. In most cases, these take the form of four-line stanzas, where the second and fourth lines rhyme. The length varies from a single stanza to ten or more. Decide on your target outlet, and make the length of your verse story and the age group to which it will appeal compatible with the market.

8

WRITING SLOGANS

Entering competitions is an important part of the writing life of many shorts specialists. Some writers have repeated success which has nothing to do with luck.

You will find competitions advertised all over the place. It is difficult to pick up a newspaper, go shopping or even just watch television without hearing of new ones. Junk mail is crammed with letters advising you that you might have won a car, holiday or vast sum in cash.

If you are planning to enter any competition, begin by reading the rules in detail. It is a waste of time and effort to submit an entry after the closing date, or without your name and address on it, or without the essential qualifiers of, say, proof of purchase of some product and the accompanying till receipt. Consider the different options you will find.

Some competitions are no more than a lottery. A number is selected by computer, or a ticket is picked out of a hat. It is always worth entering these, as long as you do not put yourself to any trouble or expense by doing so. Sheer luck is involved, but somebody has to be lucky. Enter them with the same degree of latent excitement with which you would check off your premium bond numbers if you knew you had only the minimum holding. You will not be disappointed, and there is always that remote chance of a win.

Another category of competition requires you to construct a list. You might be asked to write down in order of importance the safety features quoted concerning a new car. Or perhaps you are asked which elements contribute most to the success of a family holiday.

The answers to these competitions will always have a degree

of subjectivity about them. In the first example, it would make sense to study the advertising material produced by the car manufacturer. If it places the strongest emphasis on the reliability of a revolutionary new braking device, that is likely to be high in the list of safety features. If it gives only a passing mention to the style of seat belts used, this feature will probably be lower on the list.

The second example is more arbitrary. We all have different ideas about family holidays. For some, sandy beaches where adults can play with the children are vital; others would prefer a babysitting service.

At the end of the day, your subjective assessments have to be in agreement with the judge's. Although there is a degree of skill and thinking involved, luck plays a major part. Again, enter if you have nothing to lose by doing so.

By far the most interesting competitions are those which demand some skill or knowledge. You might have to answer questions on a particular topic, to pair book titles with authors, to identify anonymous locations on a map, etc.

If you are going to enter, the assumption is that you are totally accurate in the knowledge elements. There is no point in wasting a stamp if you are not sure whether you have matched the capitals to the countries correctly, or counted the right number of differences between one picture and another almost identical one.

Getting the right answers is the easy part. Practically everyone who entered will have managed this. The real challenge comes with the tie-breaker, where you have to create a winning slogan.

This is where your skills as a shorts writer are put to their ultimate test. You are trying to create a phrase which will capture the attention of a judge or panel of judges. Every other entrant will be doing the same. Good is not good enough. It is up to you to ensure that your entry is the best.

When producing slogans there are general guidelines which you should follow to give yourself a reasonable chance:

● Make sure you are answering the right question. If a tie-breaker depends on your assessment of the reasons why Brand X is the product leader, an explanation of your personal reason for buying it will not win.

- Keep to the word limit. Your slogan assessing Brand X's qualities may be stunning, but if it is written in eleven words instead of ten it cannot be successful.
- Make sure your slogan is memorable. It must grab the judge and insist on being heard – and remembered.
- Strive for originality. Every other entrant in competition with you is working from the same starting point. Look for the unusual angle that will surprise and delight.
- Make a conscious effort to absorb the techniques of advertising slogans. This is not a suggestion that you should produce a re-hash of a company's advertising material. But these slogans are the ones for which the company pays huge sums of money simply because they are so effective. A clever phrase which becomes synonymous with a product is the corporate dream. A good ear for a similar clever phrase may win you the competition.

The Product-Related Slogan

In this tie-breaker, you are required to make a statement about a product or service. You may have to complete a sentence which begins:

> I always choose this product because . . .

or you may have to construct the entire sentence.

This is one of the most common formulas for tie-breakers, as it has great appeal and by its nature suggests that absolutely anyone can attempt it. It is not uncommon for hundreds of thousands of entries to be received.

The winning entry is likely to be complimentary about the product. Think of all the nice things you can find to say about it. Think quickly, jotting down every idea that occurs to you.

You might say that the product is reasonably priced, and good value; that its consistently high quality is excellent; that your Granny used to use it. Keep pouring the flow of ideas onto the paper.

Pause for thought after a couple of minutes. Now push your list of ideas to one side. If they were the first things to enter your mind, they will have entered a good proportion of the other minds being applied to the same task.

Delve a little more deeply. How do you visualise the product? Is it associated in your mind with nostalgia, with lively groups of people, with solitude, with sex? There may be no logical reason for your assessment. Do not worry. Believe in your instinct. You will have absorbed the subliminal messages carried by the product's advertising.

Channel your ideas through these associations. Make another list of thoughts bearing them in mind. You will be edging towards the message the product manufacturers are trying to put across.

Add to this more useful list the key words connected with the product name and the prize.

Experiment with all the words you have written down on this paper. Try them in different phrase groupings, and then change their order within the phrases. Do you find anything that looks familiar? Sometimes a saying appears which sounds similar to a common expression. There might be a play on words or a pun within it. Look out for any literary devices which are emerging.

As an example, suppose that you are writing about a product called Crumbles Biscuits. You have already rejected the list of comments which remind you of the facts about the product, and your mundane first thoughts. Your second list reflects the jokey nature of their advertising. The holiday prize is illustrated by a picture of palm trees and coconuts.

This second list might read:

oh crumbs
crumbling crunchies
coconut crunch/crumbs
catch a coconut
catch a falling coconut
palm oil
greasing the palm   —   etc. etc.

Most of this material will be dropped, of course. A study of all the phrases shows a lot of use of the letter 'c.' It might be worth exploring an alliterative effect:

Crumbly Crumbles create coconutty crunches.

or:

Catch a coconut to capture a Crumbles moment.

In order to highlight the alliteration, play about with the idea of tongue-twisters. Now go back to the nature of the statement required in the tie-breaker.

I always choose Crumbles Biscuits because ...

and you might choose to complete it with:

Crunching a Crumbles creates the crispiest coconut crumbs.

Every list will offer you a new device for creating your tie-breaking slogan. The knack of identifying and capitalising on the device will edge you towards success.

Name Slogans

Some competitions require you to invent a new word to give a title to something. You may have to name a dish for which you are given the recipe, or christen a fictitious island.

As before, abandon your initial ideas. Think about all the facets of the object, and see how you can combine them into a single word. Keep your mind open to acronyms, and to words whose similar sounds will create the right impression in the reader's mind.

Suppose you are naming a recipe which places pork chops and apples in a Somerset cider sauce. Think of all the associated words:

pork chops
apples

cider
scrumpy
Somerset
delicious
palatable
tasty

Play about with the different syllables in the words, and you might come up with a combination like 'Scrumchops', merging the idea of rough cider with the chops. As this word sounds a little like 'scrumptious' you are reinforcing the message of something good to eat.

You will notice that most of the words in the list have been ignored. This is inevitable. If you tried to incorporate every facet of your object, you would end up with an unpronounceable monstrosity.

Minimal Clue Slogans

Some competitions ask more from their tie-breakers by giving only the subject heading for the required slogan, without going into details. You may have to offer a tip, a safety hint, a cocktail recipe, or your own ideas about a broad subject, such as your perfect night out. You will often find a more generous word limit allowed to this style of slogan.

Although other shorts give you the scope for recycling ideas, in this case you must come up with something totally original.

For a tip, think back to the first time you realised there was an easier way of performing a task. Did you get the idea from an article or a broadcast? Did someone else make the suggestion to you? Or did it suddenly occur to you that a certain practice would make life easier?

Only consider your tip as a potential winner if it falls into the last category. If it does not, another competitor is bound to have suggested it, and you will lose any points you might have gained for originality.

With tips and hints you have a choice as to whether to restrict your comments to a limited area of interest, or to offer a piece of general advice. The restricted comment is more likely to be unique. Take this culinary tip, for example:

> Use mayonnaise as a delicious thickener for casseroles.

This is similar advice to:

> Just before serving, stir a tablespoon of mayonnaise into a pot of chilli con carne. Swirl it into the chilli, then serve immediately.

The second version sounds more exotic and so may catch the judge's imagination.

The same technique can be adapted easily. If you were asked to provide a hint for safety in the home, you could say:

> Keep all medicines out of the reach of children.

You would make more impact by saying:

> Keep all medicines in a first aid box with a secure lid, and take the further precaution of storing the box on a high shelf where it is hidden from children's view.

You might lose something in terms of a snappy delivery, but you will make the reader think.

The request for a description of a perfect night out, or the choice of an ideal dinner partner, preferred holiday destination etc. is going to require a subjective opinion. It is also going to make for a popular competition. Everyone who has a modicum of imagination will be intrigued and want to enter. You must strive to make your suggestion memorable for a reason other than the one implied in the challenge.

A perfect night out, for example, could be seen in terms of a piece of music. You could have the overture of a romantic meeting and the slow passage of a first kiss. There could be arpeggios of canapés and chromatics of champagne. The allegro of a visit to the theatre could be followed by the final crashing chords of however you'd like the evening to end.

Have the same fun with the dinner companion idea. It might be facetious to suggest that Oscar Wilde would be the perfect partner, as he would be wittier from beyond the grave than anyone else you know could be this side of it. Then again, it might not.

The Cartoon Caption

If you are presented with a cartoon picture to which you have to add comment, keep it short and simple. Examine the picture carefully, and ask yourself precisely what you are seeing.

The picture may indicate that a character is speaking. If this is the case, what is going on and affecting that character? Who else is present? What has the character been doing all day, and just a moment ago, and what will happen next?

If no character is pictured open-mouthed, you can ascribe words to anyone depicted, or even to an unseen presence. As long as it is perfectly clear who is speaking, feel free to use dialogue.

Sometimes dialogue is not required, and the caption is a comment. You should still scrutinise the cartoon minutely, and look for a possible double meaning in something portrayed there. Tap into every style of humour which might fit.

Try out various ideas to see which is exactly right and appropriate to every aspect of the picture. When you are completely satisfied, put the cartoon away for a couple of days, and then get it out and compare it with your caption. If it makes you laugh aloud, send it off at once. If you are still pleased with it, fine. If you cannot understand why it is supposed to be funny, go back to the drawing-board.

Unless you are submitting your caption immediately before the competition's deadline, try to avoid topical allusions. Otherwise today's up-to-the-minute news and unforgettable scandals will be forgotten history before your masterpiece reaches the judge.

Verse Tie-Breakers

Some tie-breakers take the form of a rhyme or limerick which you have to complete. This is extremely difficult; not to find appropriate rhyming words, but to find different rhyming words from everybody else's.

Stretch your imagination beyond its limits. Have fun experimenting with the form of words. Allow a universally understood foreign word or phrase to creep in, unless the competition rules specifically forbid this. Relish the sounds you are creating. Make preposterous rhymes, eg:

'In Guadalajara
he played his guitarra . . .'

This is the time when you should reach for the rhyming dictionary, and be presented with lists of words which unaided brain cells might have struggled after for hours.

Words like it, bit, lit and sit rhyme perfectly together. But plummet, halfwit, Photofit and lickety-split are good fun – and stand a better chance of being original.

The more lines you have to produce to finish the verse, the more scope you have to make it uniquely yours. Adding the last line to a limerick is far more difficult to achieve with any individuality than constructing the last four after being presented with the opening one. Consider these examples:

If you were given:

A lady who lived in Japan
Declared, 'How unhappy I am!
    I've plenty of money
    But life isn't funny' . . .

you might add something like:

'Because I can't get me a man.'

Or:

And so she retired to Saipan.

70

Given no more than the initial line, you would have far wider options for continuing the limerick, eg:

A lady who lived in Japan
Liked to sunbathe and work on her tan.
　But she used her sun bed
　Till she turned lobster-red –
So she had to abandon her plan.

In your eagerness to seek out good rhymes, do not forget the metrical pattern of the poem's lines. Perfect rhyme loses all its effect if an incongruous pattern of stressed and unstressed syllables undermines the beat of the verse. Make rhyme and metre harmonious, and you may have produced a winner.

Practising Your Slogan Skills

If you enjoy competitions, be sure to exercise the skills that are needed for inventing tie-breaking slogans. You can do this any time you have a moment to yourself. Think about slogan techniques while you are mowing the lawn or driving to work.

Let your mind range over clichés, and try to twist their words to make subtle changes in the meaning.

Think about familiar catchphrases, and analyse them to see whether you can use puns to create clever sayings.

Make up verses and limericks, incorporating various products and services into the verse.

Play about with anagrams and acronyms. Recall famous quotations and then substitute a word here and there to change their meaning completely.

When you have a minute to sit quietly and concentrate, study a reference book of successful slogans, a thesaurus, or the dictionary. Play with words, manipulate and befriend them. Then the next time you need to find a good slogan, it will leap into your head with alacrity.

9

PUZZLES, QUIZZES, WORD GAMES AND QUESTIONNAIRES

There are magazines devoted entirely to puzzles of various kinds, and pages of quizzes and games in newspapers, general interest magazines and children's comics. The challenge of a puzzle is popular, and creating them can be even more pleasurable than doing them.

If you have an original idea for a brainteaser or word game, you might find an outlet willing to commission your work on a regular basis. Coming up with the idea is difficult. There is such a wide fascination with puzzles that practically everything seems to have been tried before.

You might be able to devise something new by adopting a 'mix and match' technique with a combination of these ideas. The answers to one puzzle could provide you with a set of clues for solving a different sort of puzzle.

Pitch this work at a range of levels. Just as there are television quizzes ranging from the impossibly academic to the too easy to be true, so printed puzzles should offer something for everyone.

Crosswords

The starting point for creating a crossword is the grid. This is usually symmetrical, and different outlets use grids of different sizes and patterns. Be sure you know your target market, and prepare a crossword which will be compatible with their regular grid.

It is vital to fit all the answers into a specimen grid before you start on the hard work of composing clues. Begin with the longest words or phrases, then work down through shorter and shorter ones. It is a simple matter to slot in three- and four-letter words at the end.

Remember that mutual squares in the grid will assist the solver who has answered the first clue when he is faced with the second. Consonants give more help than vowels; so when there is a choice, by fitting consonants into mutual spaces you will make your crossword a little easier.

Make your job as a compiler easier by investing in a crossword dictionary or equivalent computer programme. These provide you with all the words you will need, categorised according to number and position of letters. There are several on the market, with variations in their form of presentation. Browse through them to decide which would work best for you.

When you come to prepare the clues, aim for a constant level of difficulty throughout one puzzle. You may be asking a direct question whose answer goes straight into the puzzle, or you may be approaching from a more oblique route, with a cryptic clue. It is essential to back up your cryptic clue by reinforcement of the idea.

For example, if the answer required were 'stranger', a direct clue might be: 'Somebody you do not know'. A cryptic clue could be: 'More odd one who roams the way'. 'More odd' implies stranger, reinforced by the fact that 'The way' can be st. (short for street) and 'one who roams' a ranger.

The same answer could emerge from: 'The rest rang round, more peculiar'. 'Round' suggests the movement of letters to make an anagram, and the reinforcement would be 'more peculiar'.

You can add extra interest to your crosswords by introducing a theme into the clues. Perhaps all the signs of the zodiac could appear as answers, or different cheeses, or American states.

You can make the crossword more difficult by leaving some clues without numbers, by using the initial letter of the answer as a code for finding where that answer fits, or by throwing a rogue word as a red herring into some of the clues. Always make sure that it is possible to find a solution, or the publication where your puzzle appears will be besieged by outraged puzzle addicts.

A simple way to combine the crossword with an additional puzzle is to provide numbers in some of the spaces in addition to the ordinary clue numbering. The letters in these specially numbered squares, when placed in order, spell out a message.

A similar idea is to produce an acrostic. The answers to the clues all read horizontally, while their initial letters spell the hidden message when read vertically.

If you enjoy filling in crosswords, you will love compiling them. If not, you will probably be bored to distraction, and it would be a good idea to ignore this type of puzzle.

Wordsearches

A very simple puzzle enjoyed by both adults and children is the wordsearch. This consists of a large square (or rectangle) divided into smaller squares in which the letters appear. At first sight, it looks like a crazed jumble of letters; but as you examine it, genuine words emerge. They are often on the same theme, and appear in straight lines in all directions. The puzzle is completed when you have been able to draw a line through each of the genuine words, which are given in a separate list.

When you are compiling a wordsearch, again start with the grid. (The difference between this and the crossword grid is that there are no blanked squares.) Now make a list of words associated with any subject, eg. shells, sand, jellyfish, wave, seaweed etc.

Starting with the longest words, write each word into the grid in a straight line in any direction, ie. forwards, backwards, up, down or diagonally (upwards or downwards, along either angled plane). Add the shorter words, fitting them around and through each other. If 'jellyfish' were written across the middle of the page, 'shells' could cross it either vertically or diagonally, making use of the 'e' or an 'l'.

When you have fitted all the words from your list into the grid, fill the blank squares with random letters of the alphabet. You can make things more difficult by using the same balance of letters as we find in words, ie. more uses of a vowel than any one consonant, and more frequent repetitions of 's', 'r', 't' etc. than 'j', 'z' and 'k'.

If your wordsearch has fifteen squares by fifteen, a total of twenty words to be found is likely to take an adult 5 – 10 minutes and a child under ten 15 – 20 minutes. A larger puzzle with more words will take relatively longer to solve.

A wordsearch is often used by the local press to allocate a prize. If you undertake to produce one for your paper, find out the nature of the prize and incorporate appropriate words. The example given above would be perfect if the prize were a family rail ticket to a seaside resort. If the prize were a skateboard, hidden words such as 'road', 'wheels' and 'tarmac' would be more relevant.

Number Puzzles

Although these examples deal in words, you can always create puzzles out of numbers, using the elements of addition, subtraction, multiplication and division.

One simple form of number puzzle consists of a square subdivided into just a few smaller squares – 16 or 25 is sufficient.

You place numbers into selected small squares, and the challenge is to complete all the blanks in such a way that the sides each add up to the same number, or that the odd numbers must be adjacent to even numbers, or that the sums of each line are proportional.

This type of puzzle can be adapted for even the smallest children. You can start with something as simple as:

$4 + ? = 7.$

The ludic quality of the exercise takes all the pain out of arithmetic.

Quizzes

The challenge of answering a few direct questions is one to which most readers rise. Setting the questions is a challenge in itself. You have to be absolutely sure about the accuracy of the answers, and that there is no ambiguity in the questions.

Check puzzle magazines, and puzzle pages in general magazines and newspapers to see whether a quiz is already featured. If it is not, you can always suggest one. If it is, ask whether freelance contributions to the column are welcomed.

Your target outlet will indicate the number of questions required and the level of difficulty expected. You may choose random questions, or fit them all to a theme. Perhaps the questions relate to events which happened in a particular year, and the final task is to guess the year. Or the initial letters of each answer turn out to form a word which links the questions together.

Try to ring the changes with your questions. Even two or three of the same sort will become tedious, eg:

> In which Shakespeare play do we meet Beatrice and Benedick?
> Which Shakespeare play starts with three witches on a blasted heath?
> In which Shakespeare play does the main character drown his books?

It would be much more interesting if you changed your approach for the second two questions:

> Who and where are the three characters who open *Macbeth*?
> What does Prospero drown in *The Tempest*?

Quizzes are often presented just for fun, and the answers given on another page. If the quiz takes the form of a competition, make it clear that the winner will be first out of the hat. The publication will be inundated with replies.

Brain Teasers

These can take the form of mathematical puzzles, anagrams and snippets of all sorts. They might pose a genuine problem, eg:

> Three brothers were born with three years between each. The sum
> of their ages equals their mother's age. She was 19 when her

eldest son was born. How old are they all now?
(In case you are wondering, the answer is 8, 11, 14 and 33 years.)

They might present a 'red herring' problem, eg:

On January 1, 1961, a plane crashed over the border between England and Wales. The cockpit and black box landed on the English side, but the bulk of the wreckage fell over Wales. In which country were the survivors buried?
(Nowhere. Only the dead were buried.)

Anagrams are fascinating to devise. There might be a simple question:

In which town do LEECHES DRIFT?
(Chesterfield.)

Or something more complicated:

How do MOTHERS kill ONCE EVIL sons?
(They SMOTHER them with VIOLENCE.)

Riddles are not only intended to entertain children. They may be included with material for adults:

What is the difference between an author and a carnivore with a taste for unusual game?
One writes books, and the other bites rooks.

And the sillier the better:

What is the difference between an elephant and a pillar box? –
I've no idea.
Well, that's the last time I send you to post a letter.

Another brain teaser seeks the linking factor in a group of words or phrases, eg:

iron, Saddleback, children's ball game
(pig – pig iron, breed of pig, pig in the middle)

You can ask for the three-letter word which can be added to certain other words to create new words, eg:

– – –pet   Red – – –   – – –case
(car)

You can look for a chain to change one word into another. The idea is to alter one letter at a time, forming a complete word of four letters at every stage. For example:

change CLAN into SHOP
(clan – clap – clop – chop – shop)

You can challenge the participant to make as many words as possible out of a certain word. Set a few rules. For instance, each letter may be used once only in each word; words must have at least four letters; plurals may not be used; foreign words and proper nouns are excluded. To make the test more difficult, you can impose the condition that all words must contain a certain letter. For example, 'SPRINTER (all words must contain 'r')' could produce 'rent, print, printer, spire, trip, tripe, rite' . . . but not, of course, 'spine'.

It is a good idea to impose targets for people to achieve, perhaps by saying that 10 words is average, 20 is good, 30 is excellent.

Add to your list of brain teasers by letting your mind range in its idle moments over all the possibilities of language. Get together with another shorts writer to increase your experience of this form of puzzle, and you will find the ideas flowing more quickly than you can harness them.

Word Games

If you are familiar with traditional party games, you will probably know a store of word games which can be adapted for publication.

The following challenging idea is one of the simplest to produce. It depends on the link between numbers and words. The numbers are given, and the words are presented in initials, eg:

12 D.O.C.	(days of Christmas)
16 O.I.A.P.	(ounces in a pound)
T. 39 S.	(*The 39 Steps*)
12 M.O.A.J.	(members of a jury)
52 C.I.A.P.	(cards in a pack)
A.T.W.I. 80 D.	(*Around the World in 80 Days*)

One mathematical word game depends on people's knowledge of slang terms, and skills in lateral thinking. You create a sum, and the player has to work out the elements to be added together and then complete the sum. This idea uses money. Ask the player to add 'a pony' (£25), 'a pair of knickers' (£2), and 'a crown' (25p). The answer would be £27.25. Make the clues as simple or as cryptic as you like. Use pre-decimal slang and currency for total confusion.

Another word game muddles the word order of familiar sayings, eg:

Light hands make work many.
(Many hands make light work.)

Or you can put the wrong halves of sayings together, and challenge the player to sort them out:

A bird in the hand gathers no moss.
Stone walls is not gold.
All that glisters is worth two in the bush.
A rolling stone do not a prison make.

These are soon disentangled to read:

A bird in the hand is worth two in the bush.
Stone walls do not a prison make.
All that glisters is not gold.
A rolling stone gathers no moss.

Four examples make this an easy exercise. Use ten or a dozen sayings, and you create a real challenge.

Another game depends on the player's ability to spot clues. You provide an ultra short story describing a crime. There are several possible solutions, but the clues concealed in the story indicate the true pattern of events. The reader has to follow the clues to their logical conclusion, and can then solve the mystery.

The idea of crossed telephone lines is used in one game. There are three conversations (involving six speakers) going on at the same time. The reader is presented with a jumble of sentences, and has to sort them into order in three columns to produce three coherent conversations.

Another version of this is to take three familiar poems (or stanzas) and jumble the lines from them so they are all mixed together and printed in the wrong order. The reader has to sort them out.

Every family has its own set of pen and paper games which could be adapted as challenges for an individual player, and published as such. Your only problem is that your own list of games is finite. Compare notes with friends to discover a new range of games, and you have a whole lot more to adapt.

'Psychology' Questionnaires

Do not let this title put you off. You do not have to be a psychologist to set this form of short, nor do you have to be in need of psychoanalysis to work through it. It is set and completed just for fun, and should never be taken any more seriously than that.

The idea is to provide a lighthearted look at some aspect of the subject's character. By assessing reactions to certain situations, you come to a number of conclusions.

For example, a magazine aimed at teenage girls might feature one of these questionnaires asking: 'How well do you get on with people?' Questions could include:

Your best friend starts going out with your boyfriend. Do you:
a) tell her you never want to speak to her again?
b) tell him you never want to speak to him again?
c) ignore it, as you really like them both?

Your Mum refuses to let you go out in the evening when you have to be at school the next day. Everyone else's mother agrees to let them out. Do you:

a) storm out of the house without telling Mum you're going?
b) ask again to go, if you promise to be home by ten?
c) turn sulky and bad-tempered, and refuse to speak to anyone?

When the subject has answered a dozen or so questions, you draw the conclusions. You can do this in one of two ways. You can ask the subject whether she scored mostly a, b or c, or a complete mixture, and then write an assessment for each possible response. Or you can award a number of points for each of the answers to every question. Again, give assessments, but use the basis of scores of 'under 12', '13-24', 'over 25' to guide your subject.

The questionnaire is not limited to youngsters. You could devise one for a women's magazine on a theme such as: 'What sort of a hostess are you?' Here a typical question might be:

You have guests coming to dinner. Do you:
a) insist on producing a culinary masterpiece for every course, and spend the whole evening in the kitchen?
b) plan a meal which allows you plenty of time to chat with the guests?
c) go to the local supermarket and buy the full range that you can throw into the microwave?

Again, a sequence of questions leads to a choice of conclusions, preferably to be taken with a pinch of salt.

You can make the questionnaire a little more complex by creating it for two people, eg. on a theme of: 'How well do you know your partner?' In this case, you can ask the same questions but produce two sets of answers. Or you can ask ten questions for one partner to answer on the other's behalf, and then another ten for the second partner to answer on behalf of the first. Drawing these results together can be rather complicated, but the exercise is rewarding. As it is more unusual, it has a better chance of acceptance by your chosen outlet.

10

SPECIALISING

It is useful for a writer, particularly one who produces non-fiction, to be identified with a specific area of subject-matter. Shorts writers are no exception. Write frequently about your chosen topic, and you will become synonymous with it.

Your chosen topic is likely to reflect another of your interests. Perhaps you love flowers. It would be logical to concentrate on flowers when writing shorts. Your output might consist of:

- readers' letters about gifts of flowers, the delightful sensation of walking through wildflowers, anecdotes concerning flowers and flower arranging
- tips on creating artistic displays, how to make cut flowers last
- fillers on the language of flowers
- verses about flowers
- quizzes and puzzles using the common link of flowers.

By doing this you are combining your special interest with your love of writing. One element which will be present in this combination is enthusiasm. Your writing is likely to have that extra indefinable quality which gladdens the reader, and which arises from your genuine feelings.

With only a modicum of widening into other areas, you can expand on your subject matter. Maybe you can include lawns, houseplants, trees and wildlife. You are not really moving out of your sphere of interest, but enriching your experience of it, along with your reader's.

File with care the writing you produce. Writers should never throw anything away, and this is doubly important for the non-fiction writer. There are always further avenues to explore using the same material, bearing in mind that there is no copyright on facts you have quoted, only on the pattern of words you have used to convey the facts.

Leave your files of work alone for a few months, and then go through them again, checking whether there is any further mileage in an old idea, or whether you are inspired to produce a new one.

Look back at your original list of writings. You could produce new readers' letters from events which have occurred since you last wrote; or your reflections on the changing seasons, and how they affect wildflowers; or the pleasure you bring by buying someone a bunch of flowers.

You could create some new tips, suggesting unusual containers for flowers, for example, or describing how to place a display beside a picture or mirror to enhance its effect.

Make a different list of flowers whose meanings you can describe in a filler. Look at the references to flowers in history and mythology. Explore those through fillers, too.

Go back to your original list of flower-meanings and write a poem about any one of them.

Undertake a new project, such as a study of the flora of a different country, and expand your scope as a writer while your knowledge is growing.

In other words, you can return to your chosen areas an infinite number of times, and find new information, clever combinations of ideas, and different ways to convey your expertise. Specialising does not have to be restrictive.

Diversifying

Although this is the opposite of specialising, you can indulge in diversification at the same time. As we have seen, concentration on areas of subject matter in which you have a special interest is useful. Producing blocks of shorts, such as a dozen readers' letters at a sitting, is an efficient use of time.

Variety of approach, however, brings its own freshness to your writing. So having spent an hour on your pet subject, or a block of shorts in one style, go back to your desk with your mind wide open.

The shorts writer and the poet share a special privilege. They have the opportunity to tackle a brand new area of material in an entirely different way every time they sit down to write.

Diversifying involves you in the fascinating practice of learning about new things. Spend part of your writing period absorbing new information from books, radio and television, or merely through observation. Everything you absorb is filtered through your own imagination and experience, ready to be communicated via your writing.

To keep your approach really dynamic, do not start the day with any preconceived ideas. Browse through the media until something inspires you to produce a short. Write it – and then go back to the browsing.

This is not the most time-effective way of working, but the sense of refreshment provided by this approach is a revitalising agent which should not be underestimated.

Finding New Outlets

No matter how successful you are in placing your shorts, always keep your eyes open for new market opportunities. You are already submitting work to existing columns and, where appropriate, suggesting ideas for additional ones. Watch for new magazines coming onto the bookshelves. Their editors might be particularly receptive to your suggestions. Watch, too, for magazines which are re-launched, or which change their appearance. They could be ripe for a fresh approach.

Consider that everything which appears in print has been written by somebody. Someone constructed the pages that appear on your Teletext. Someone composed the instruction leaflet for your washing machine. Someone decided on the wording of your theatre programme.

Obviously, in many instances these people are employed by the relevant company to do the work. But ask yourself how many examples could have been produced by a freelance writer, and you may be surprised by your own answer. That freelance writer could be you. The variety of approach you need for producing shorts gives you the flexibility to apply yourself to any writing project.

Take every opportunity you can to secure a niche for yourself and your shorts. You are increasing the potential interest in your work, and approaching it with a professional attitude.

Taking the Longer View

In essence, this book deals only with shorts, but it would be silly to ignore the potential for expanding such material in order to create further writing outlets. This is where the advice to keep a copy of everything you write becomes an imperative.

Look again at the accumulation of material on which you still hold the copyright. Experiment by grouping it together in different ways, and think carefully about its potential.

You might, for example, have produced fifty tips over a period of time. Why not contact your local paper to see whether they would feature them as a weekly column, printing five or six tips at once?

Having established the column, collect all the tips you can to keep it going. If it looks in danger of flagging, solicit further material from readers of the paper.

One writer who did this went on to produce a complete non-fiction book of tips, listed under categories such as 'cleaning', 'cookery', etc. to make it easier for the reader to find the necessary advice.

Compiling a full-length article is a good way of re-using shorts. They can be grouped together in a logical order with linking material to join them. If you are list-minded, use the format of a set number of tips or an alphabet.

A brief introductory paragraph is all you need, apart from the tips themselves. Look at this simple example:

Ten Tips for Painless Children's Parties

Does your child's approaching birthday fill you with dread? Do you feel you cannot cope with the massed invasion of six-year-olds? Follow this advice, and it will be easier than you think.

1 Plan the games you will play and the order in which they will be played. Keep all the materials together, ready for use, and out of the reach of the guests.
2 Start by giving each child a bag with his or her name on. This can be used to collect items to be found in the first game, and afterwards to accumulate prizes, cake etc.
3 Set out the children's teas in individual portions. It saves having to pass sandwiches around and across the table, and

ensures that everyone gets a fair share of special treats.

Continue in this vein, and before you know it, you have a complete article. The alphabet technique is almost the same:

An ABC of Beauty

Follow all the advice from A to Z for a more confident, beautiful you.

A Aromatherapy. Treat yourself to an occasional massage, and use aromatherapy oils in your bath.
B Blusher. Be sure to blend it in for a natural appearance to avoid the 'painted doll' effect.
C Colouring. Experiment with different shades for eyes and lips, but do not forget that your skin tone dictates the colours you will be able to wear most easily.

Remember that you will probably have to cheat by the time you get to the end. Do not abandon your idea if you cannot find anything for 'x' and 'y'. You will be able to get away with something as silly as 'Xercise is good for you' or 'Y not try this for . . .'

If you have produced a lot of quizzes for odd issues of magazines, why not offer them as a set? The same applies to brainteasers, puzzles etc.

Be sure to divide this sort of work into degrees of difficulty. A book containing quizzes for seven-year-olds and for adults is neither one thing nor the other. If you have written at both of those levels, you have the material for two different books.

You do not have to have produced hundreds of shorts for this to be a viable idea. Look at the pocket-sized puzzle, joke and game books you can buy. The publishers of these are looking for much less material than the publisher of a full-length puzzle book.

If verse is your special interest, have you thought of putting together a collection of your rhyming poetry? Again, publishers are willing to consider slender volumes in this area – you do not have to provide sheaves of poems.

Work which can be categorised may receive a special welcome, not least because there is the scope for a series of booklets to be produced. Imagine a collection of half a dozen books with maybe only sixteen pages in each. Attractive illustrations and meaningful poems could be geared to a particular readership. For example, there could be a booklet of inspirational verses, poems to raise a smile, a 'glad to be alive' booklet, a 'wonders of nature' booklet, etc.

This type of publication sells in bookshops, newsagents and card shops. If you did not find a publisher who was interested, you might even consider publishing it yourself, and taking your material directly to a printer.

This course of action would involve you in some expense and planning, but is highly rewarding. If you wish to pursue the idea, do consult Peter Finch's 'How to Publish your Poetry' (Allison and Busby) before you begin.

You might find a whole new career, publishing all sorts of shorts, including mini-sagas and ultra short stories, by yourself and by other authors. Remember, though, that you cannot count on making your fortune. If you are very lucky, your self-publishing ventures might break even.

The beauty of these techniques is that you do not have to sacrifice the shorts writing you enjoy in order to produce longer works. An added bonus is that publication in article and book form brings you recognition as a writer which you may not have experienced when your shorts appeared individually.

The advantage of this recognition is twofold. Success breeds success, and when your name is recognised it helps you to sell more of your work. You also become acknowledged as an expert, and your advice, comments and possibly even skills as a speaker may be solicited.

Motivation

All writers have to be self-motivated. Nobody stands over you with a stopwatch making sure that you work efficiently. There is no time clock to ensure you are at your desk at a set time. If you fail to write, the world does not end. The worst that can happen is that the editor hoping to use your work uses somebody else's instead.

If you are going to be a writer, the harsh fact is that you have to write. Some people have an airy notion of writers swanning around waiting for inspiration. Real writers know they need discipline.

Assuming that you genuinely want to write, it is a good idea to find your own way of exerting discipline. One of these suggestions might help.

Decide on the level of earnings you hope your writing will produce. Be realistic. Shorts are written for pocket money, not fortunes.

Work out the proportion of your submissions which is statistically likely to be accepted. Ensure that you send out every week or every month enough material to allow for rejections but still yield your target earnings.

For example, say you are hoping to earn £100 in a set period of time. You know that on average a third of your writing will be accepted and two thirds ignored or rejected. You will need to submit enough material to earn £300 (if it were all accepted) in order to be likely to earn your target of £100.

Using a different angle of approach, decide how long you want to spend on your writing. Be realistic, basing your target on the spare time at your disposal. Allow yourself some time off.

For example, you might feel that you could give an hour every day, seven days a week. This would leave you without any days off. Decide instead to write for an hour a day on five days of the week.

Professional or domestic circumstances, such as overtime at work, or the need to complete some household task, may intervene. If they prevent you from working for your hour, do not worry. Start with a clean slate the next day, aiming once again to write for an hour. If, however, laziness or apathy keeps you from the desk, add the hour you have wasted to the next day's allocation and make up for the lost time.

Another way of keeping a watch on your output is to make a list at the beginning of the week or month of the things you intend to write during that period. This is especially useful for writers who do not have a fixed pattern of other work, and so have irregular time slots available.

You might list ten letters, six fillers, two puzzle pages, three verses etc. Each time you start to write, examine your own frame of mind first and select the piece of writing with which you feel you would be most in tune.

If you get to the end of your writing list well within the time period, you have underestimated either the time at your disposal or the speed at which you work. If you have lots left to do at the end of your time allocation, carry it forward into the next period. If you always have the same elements left on the list, presumably they are the shorts you least enjoy writing. Cut down on them when you prepare your next list, and substitute additional shorts of the kind you prefer.

Whichever technique you use, be sure to keep records for two reasons. When we looked at readers' letters the need for record-keeping was explained. It is essential to keep a note of all the shorts you have sent out, where you sent them and the eventual result.

The second reason is to be aware of the level of work you are accomplishing. One of the disadvantages of working with shorts is that your published work is usually in an ephemeral format. You do not have a thick book to hold in your hand; nor can you go and watch the play you wrote in performance. Instead your work seems to disappear into the ether.

If you keep a note of every letter you send or competition you enter, you will have a record that pleases you at least as much as the bank balance and the prizes you are amassing.

Finding your motivation is important, but the most useful motivation is the real desire to write. If that is missing, take up another interest. Life is too short to be devoted to the arduous task of writing if your heart and soul are not in it.

Final Comment

Whatever direction your writing life takes, never underestimate the value of producing shorts. Practise the techniques of writing with brevity and concision, and all your writing projects are enhanced.

Submit your shorts in a professional manner, and note how the acceptances come rolling in.

Be aware that you are involved in a form of writing which brings relaxation and pleasure to many readers. Be proud of this form of writing. Talk about it, and share your enjoyment with others.

May your writing bring you every success.

INDEX